SPEAKING

YOUR

BEST

This book is dedicated to my parents, to my wonderful aunt Kate, and to my beautiful wife Audrey.

-Kevin Boland

"Every good coach stresses the fundamentals. That's what you get from Kevin in *Speaking Your Best*. If you want to improve your speaking skills, get this book."

-Bob Mori, Pastor
Sacramento Asian American Ministries

"After just a few minutes of reading this book, I learned some valuable tips about giving presentations. Each chapter contains instructions on a specific area of public speaking. This organizational style enables me to use it as a reference book to get information quickly and easily. I recommend *Speaking Your Best* to both beginners, and experienced public speakers."

-Joseph E. Giansante, MME, MIT,
MBA, U.C.L.A.
Group Product Manager, Intuit, Inc.

"Excellent organization! Clarity is the strength of the book. You cover the basics that are the foundation of good presentations."

-Frank Jamieson, President
Jamieson Advertising, Inc.
Certified Toastmaster

"Written with compassion, understanding, and a sincere desire to help others overcome their fears about public speaking."

-Hal Hester
Insurance Salesman

"A good, concise book for beginners. Kevin has a wonderful and witty writing style that captivates the reader."

"Your tip on memorizing speech openings was just the trick I needed to ease my nervousness."

Contents

Introduction

What do you do for a living? Are you employed in private business, in government, or in academia? Are you new to the workforce or a veteran? Do you manage people or are you a technical specialist? Whatever you do, chances are good you will have to speak to an audience someday. This experience could be fun and rewarding if you know some basic tips about public speaking. How can learning these simple rules help you?

First, once you learn how to organize a speech you will have little to fear when the big day arrives. Organization is the most important public speaking skill to learn. That is why it is the only subject covered in chapter one. Here you will be given an easy-to-use outline that works for any subject.

Second, many people learn how to be good at their jobs, but very few know how to speak persuasively. Those wise ones who do, get promoted into management, or start their own companies, or become consultants, or succeed at being the best in their field. Any smart businessperson will confess to you in a heartbeat that *"how you say something is as equally important as what you say."* Learning to speak persuasively has furthered many individual's careers and it can for you too.

Finally, there is an incredible metamorphosis in someone when they learn to articulate their thoughts persuasively. Suddenly, their energy and their self confidence grows. When they speak to others their enthusiasm is contagious and people believe in them. The quality of their life improves because they can now work and communicate with others in ways previously unimaginable. You can experience this change to by learning how to speak effectively.

Every public speaking book is different. Is my book the best choice for you? Let me describe the book's contents so you can make an informed decision.

What's *unique* about this book?

There are three unique qualities about this book that sets it apart from others.

First: this book is a genuine instructional guide. Instead of only telling you what to do, this handbook provides clear examples showing you how to do it. You will find an easy-to-use outline in chapter one. You'll be shown methods that actors use to give great performances in chapter three. Want to overcome your fear of speaking before groups? Read chapter two. How do you present statistics effectively? Read chapter eight. Each chapter in this book focuses on a specific speaking skill and provides clear instructions so you can master that skill.

Second: this book is reader friendly. "Easy to read" is the comment I hear most from people who have read this book. I use concrete words and easy to follow instructions in each chapter. Specific techniques are clearly explained. Paragraph transitions are smooth. Every sentence is concise. My philosophy is simple: easy reading means easy learning.

Third: this book is for beginners. You will find the fundamentals covered thoroughly. How to organize your presentation, how to use visuals, voice techniques, gesturing, how to open and close your talks, dealing with fear, and much more!

Now you know what is unique about this book. Study it, practice public speaking, and you will soon be speaking your best.

Kevin Boland
Author

Chapter 1

The beef: outlining your presentation

This chapter contains a tool that will help you give persuasive presentations. You will be surprised how easily it works. It's a mental challenge for everyone to outline a winning presentation. You can do it if you follow my advice. Organization is one of the keys to making a persuasive delivery. It is especially important for beginners because it helps you stay on track from start to finish. I have seen many speakers stand up and look intelligent, but two minutes into their talk everyone realizes they are jumping from one subject to another without smooth transitions, and they wind up looking foolish. Follow my outline exactly and you will avoid this problem. My technique works for any subject! When you sit down to organize your presentation the first step is to examine this formula.

> Step 1. Win their attention
> Step 2. Choose 3-5 meaningful subject areas
> Step 3. Select your statistics and facts
> Step 4. Draw your conclusion

Keep the above outline in front of you so it is visible. Now you are ready to start.

Win their attention

Write down under the heading "Win their attention" a few sample openings that will make them sit up and listen. You want to start off with a good first impression. Your opening must be unique and tie into the rest of the talk. What can you say to startle them? Think about three ideas and commit them to paper. The next day you can return and choose the best of the three. Limit your opening to a few sentences. Below are some sample openings showing you how to apply step number one. Let's examine them:

Poor Opening

"Today I will tell you about the function and organizational structure of my accounting department and how it makes its contribution to the company's goals."

Good Opening

"What do the bean counters do in accounting besides play with numbers? You will be surprised to hear this: we sell the company to the world! Our banks and our shareholders need quarterly guarantees that all is well at McDennys."

Poor Opening

"I will show you today how weak the plaintiff's case is. Every assertion he has made is wrong."

Good Opening

"It's incredible how weak the plaintiff's case is! Each one of his assertions is groundless."

Poor Opening

"I want to remind everyone that there are five important issues that we need to address today, so I would like to get the meeting going as quickly as possible."

Good Opening

"We have five issues on the agenda today so let's get going".

Can you see the difference between the poor and good openings? The good ones have two things in common. They use better word choice and they get right to the point. Usually, but not always, the best openings are shorter too. Read the first example of a poor opening and compare it to the first example of a good opening. The first one sounds like it's going to be a boring presentation from someone in the accounting department. The phrases, "function and organizational structure" are tiresome and worn out cliches. The second opening sounds vibrant. It promises that an interesting and animated presentation is coming. In the second example the difference between the two openings is that the good one uses better word choices. Instead of saying only that the plaintiff's case is weak, the good speaker states, "it's incredible how weak it is." Instead of simply saying his assertions are wrong, the good speaker chose the word, "groundless."

In the third example the effectiveness of the good opening over the poor one is obvious. The good opening is shorter and gets to the point quickly. The poor opening has thirty words; the good opening has only twelve.

Intelligent people do not waste words; they say what is on their minds without being long winded. You must do the same! Write openings that are concise and choose colorful words that make an impact.

Here are three more techniques to help you get your presentations off to a persuasive start.

Ask a smart question

Audiences always respond well when you start by asking a meaningful question. Asking a question forces your audience to think. It wakes people up! Your question must be related to the purpose of your talk. For example, suppose I were giving a presentation on the effect automobile airbags have on preventing fatalities. My opening question might be:

"Doesn't $1,500.00 sound like a lot of money to install a nine-inch airbag in your car?"

My listeners would probably agree that $1,500.00 is a lot of money, but after I showed them how many deaths will be prevented with airbags, most would feel it is worth the cost. Using this rhetorical question is a smart way to begin because it forces my listeners to think. Ask your audience a question! Force them to think right away and they will respect you for it. Let's examine a second method to begin your presentations.

Tell a story

Telling a story at the start of your talk is another way to win people's attention. People like stories. Stories are popular because they tug at people's hearts. A good question forces people to think; a good story forces them to feel. You do not have to tell a story at the beginning of your talk either. A good story in the middle or end of a presentation works magic too. But if you want to win their attention right away, starting out with a good story will do it. Keep your story brief. Deliver it with a lot of animation. You will be amazed at the results!

When you outline your talk, try and think of one meaningful story that illustrates a point. For example, suppose I were giving my talk entitled "Auto Airbags: Are They Worth the Cost?" I would definitely reach people's hearts and win them to my way of thinking if I told a simple but true story like this one:

"I can think of one good reason to demand that car manufacturers install an airbag in every car. Her name is Lisa Roberts. Lisa is a nine-year-old girl who wants to be a teacher when she grows up. Lisa is lucky because her dream almost perished last Fall. She was riding home from school with her mom when a drunken driver smashed into them. If the airbag had not exploded and cushioned her from smashing into the windshield, Lisa might have died."

Can you see how one good story can deliver your message? The best stories are true ones. Let's examine a third technique to jump-start your presentations.

Tell an anecdote

The dictionary defines the word anecdote as, "A short account of some interesting or humorous incident." The only real difference between a story and an anecdote is that the latter is humorous. One good anecdote can make your talk more lively! People love to laugh! It helps relieve stress. Throw in a funny anecdote and you'll score points with your audience. Here is an example of an anecdote told by a sales manager at a meeting to motivate his sales reps. The message hidden in the anecdote is that their company's fax machines are better than the competition's, and selling them is easy.

"The first time I walked into Oakland California's Highland Hospital I was in stitches. I was laughing so hard I thought I was going to choke. There were half a dozen pharmacy assistants scurrying around picking up faxes off the floor. The hospital was using their fax machines so each ward could send down orders for drugs. The pharmacy would receive the order, fill it, and send it to the ward. The fax machine they were using, the XXX brand, was so poorly designed that one out of five incoming orders fell out of the receiving tray. The assistants were spending half their workshifts bending over and picking up faxes off the floor! That is the easiest sale I ever made."

The above anecdote is brief and relevant to the needs of the audience. That's how you want yours to be! Remember the old saying "Laughter is the best medicine!" It's true, so try and come up with at least one witty anecdote in your presentations. I guarantee you will be persuasive if you do.

Don't forget! Stick to your outline and create an opening that wins the audience's attention. Use any of the three methods to open your presentation. Ask your audience a thought provoking question! Tell them a cathartic story or a witty anecdote! Create a unique opening that startles people and you'll make a good first impression. It's time now to discuss step number two.

Choose 3-5 meaningful subject areas

In this second step you will narrow down your presentation into three to five separate but related subject areas. The way you organize your talk is to break it down into its component parts. Whatever general subject you have chosen can be broken down into specific parts. Your presentation could consist of three parts or five; it just depends on how much information you need to present. In rare situations you might want to present six or seven subject areas, but be careful not to overload yourself. Most audiences will only listen to you actively for fifteen to twenty minutes. After that, they begin to think about their own problems.

Your goal now is to think about what you really want to say. Think about what the high priorities are. You must outline your presentation to meet the needs of your audience. What is in it for them? What benefits can they derive from your talk? Tell them something they don't know that will help them. Whatever your subject is, break it down into three to five specific topics. Below are some examples showing you how to apply step number two.

Presentation title: **Automobile Air bags: Are They Worth the Cost?**

A. How Air bags work as electronic systems
B. Cost of installation
C. Safety features: airbags save lives!

Above is an outline for a talk about Automobile Air bags. I broke my presentation down into three specific areas. Once I have decided that I am going to limit my presentation to these three areas the tough part is over for me. All I have to do now is choose the statistics, facts and examples to support each area. Can you see how I took the general subject of air bags and broke it down into three separate but related areas. Choose any subject! Education, religion, sports, taxes, marriage, salesmanship, T.V., and you can break it down into three to five separate but related areas.

Let's take a look at a second example.

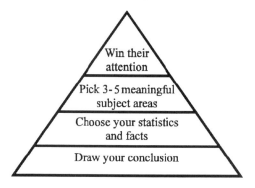

Pyramid Formula

Presentation title: **How to Market Fax Machines?**

A. Advertising: T.V., Print, Radio, Billboards
B. Direct Mail: 10% Discount Offered in the Mail
C. Sales Promotion: Sales Reps Need Extra Incentives

The above three specific areas make it easy for the speaker to organize his talk. This type of outline also makes it easy for the audience to comprehend the general subject of marketing. These subject areas were chosen because they represent the *beef* of this speaker's presentation. His goal is to describe the tactics of his marketing strategy and sell it to his audience. If he sticks to his outline, he will have a winning presentation.

The key to applying step number two is choosing the three to five relevant subject areas to talk about. Make your choices wisely. Think about what your listeners want and need to hear. I have said it before and it's worth repeating: always ask yourself, what's in it for my audience? What can I talk about that directly benefits their lives? How can I help them? If you answer these questions you will have no problem choosing the best subject areas to talk about.

Transition statements

When you move from one specific area of your presentation to another, it is critical that you let your audience know it. A lot of presentations become confusing without smooth transitions. It's easy to make your audience aware that you are closing out one part of your talk and entering into another when you use a transition statement. Here is an example:

"That about covers our advertising tactics. Unless anyone has a question, I am going to talk now about our direct marketing plans."

Do you see how easy it is? The above transition statement tells everyone that the speaker is finishing up one area and moving into another. This speaker is smart too because he gave anyone the opportunity to ask a question before switching subjects.

Here is another example:

"Don't forget to have a qualified mechanic inspect your airbag's electronic components every six months. That's all I have to say about electronics. Next I want to show you some of the safety features in a car equipped with a driver's side airbag."

Is there any doubt that the speaker is closing out one part of the presentation and switching to another? You want to state your transition statements in the same clear manner as these examples.

I don't want you to overlook the importance of using clear transition statements. People like to hear organized talks. You will keep more people interested in what you are saying when they know where you are going. Let's talk about step number three now.

Select your statistics and facts

Step number three is one of the easy ones. Choosing the right facts and statistics to present builds credibility with your audience. You show them that you did your homework. You do not need a lot of facts and statistics to support your presentation. You do need to pick wisely the ones that illustrate your points.

Common sense and good judgment apply here. Don't drown your audience with ten statistics if one good one will do. Don't give them three facts if one drives home the point adequately.

Choose one of your subject areas previously given, for example "Safety Features: Airbags Save Lives." Now you must locate any statistics or facts that support your position. You might pick this one: "Independent studies have proven that when front end collisions occur with cars equipped with airbags the occupants suffer far less serious injuries than cars equipped only with seatbelts."

If you were giving a talk on marketing fax machines, you would probably pick some statistics that show the positive effect that direct mail campaigns have on increasing sales of a given product. A good statistic to use would be "sales jumped 25% in San Francisco after our direct mail program ran in February." The important point is to choose the most meaningful statistic.

You will earn a lot of respect from your audience when you do your homework and highlight significant facts and statistics. Don't try to rush through step number three. That would be a mistake. A lot of people get lazy and their research is poor. Force yourself to think and decide which data is most important. In other words, choose the beef for your facts, not the gravy. Postpone your presentation until you've had enough time to gather the relevant data. Your audience will respect you more when you come before them fully prepared. How many people have you heard give a presentation that was full of fluff and no beef? They were foolish because they lacked the discipline to show up prepared. Keep your personal standards high. Be a winner and do your homework.

Be careful also to distinguish fact from opinion. You will be getting a lot of your facts and statistics from newspapers, magazines, and journals. Make sure when you quote someone who used a statistic that it isn't pulled from thin air. If you read that 70% of all new cars have plastic bumpers these days, be certain the 70% figure came from a legitimate research study and not the journalist's imagination. You must always know the source of your information too. In every presentation that you deliver there will be someone asking where you got your figures. If you don't know, you'll look foolish, so always be prepared to defend your numbers.

My final comment in using step number three is let wisdom, not knowledge, be your guide. What do I mean by this? Don't fire a lot of facts and statistics at your audience like a 30mm gun, hoping that if you shoot them with a barrage of data, they will be impressed. They won't. Use your common sense. Choose only those vital facts and statistics that drive home your most important points. Quality wins over quantity when it comes to using statistics wisely. Be smart and you will earn the audience's respect.

Draw your conclusion

Now you come to the final step to outlining your presentation. Your goal here is to get results. By results I mean you must have a specific purpose for giving your presentation and your conclusion has to reveal this to your audience. Like the rest of your talk, your conclusion must be brief. State your conclusion in one or two sentences. The most common mistake I see in speakers is a tendency to ramble on at the end because they don't know when to stop. They look lost because they can not think of anything else to say, so they repeat themselves. Avoid this pitfall. Don't grope around looking for insights. Write a clear closing statement and sit down!

In your final remarks, what is the one thing your audience is waiting for? They are looking for the same thing they search for when they see a movie, a play, or when they read a book: a message! That's right. They want to hear a message. They want to learn something from you so they can become wiser human beings. Your closing must be written to illustrate the purpose of your presentation and to leave the audience with a clear message.

How do you close your talk? The best technique I have seen is to sum up in one or two sentences your major conclusion. Remember writing your topic sentences in high school? The topic sentence is supposed to give your readers a clear statement of your purpose. Your conclusion must be spoken in the same way.

Below are a few examples of how to draw your conclusion and close your talk. Let's examine them:

Conclusion to, "Auto Air bags: Are They Worth the Cost!"

"As my research on auto accidents indicates, air bags save lives and reduce the number of major injuries, but only when you give them a six-month check-up by a qualified mechanic."

These closing remarks represent my purpose for giving this talk. Namely, that air bags are indeed worth the cost, but only if you maintain them properly. My purpose is to educate the audience about air bags and to make them understand the importance of safety. But suppose my purpose is different. What if I were the product manager at Ford for the Ford Escort, and I want to convince the higher-ups to put an air bag in every Escort because I believe it will increase sales? My purpose is now different, so my conclusion must be different. It might sound something like this:

"Even though making airbags standard equipment means higher manufacturing costs now, in the long term we can pass costs along to our customers, and, more importantly, it will stimulate sales of the Escort because people are buying cars now based on their safety features."

Do you see how the conclusion depends on your purpose? Make your conclusion meaningful like your high school topic sentences, and you will close intelligently.

Sometimes your conclusion not only has to be meaningful, it has to ask your audience to do something too. Many presentations are given to motivate an audience to take action.

If you are a salesman, your goal is to sell your product. If you are a church minister, you want your audience to give more of their time and money. Write your closing remarks to reflect your specific purpose. Don't be shy about coming right out and asking your audience to do something. For example:

"I think you'll agree my fax machine does everything the other ones do, but it's $500.00 less. Can I have your order?"

or how about this:

"We need to give more of ourselves to be true Christians. The more we give to others, the more we profit ourselves. Whatever you can give us today will be enormously appreciated."

or how about this closing statement:

"Ladies and Gentlemen of the jury, my client, Audrey Lee is innocent, and there is no evidence to prove otherwise. Please let her go back to her family."

In each of the above closing remarks the speaker drew the conclusion for the audience and boldly asked them to do something. Each sample close has meaning and is brief. Each one delivers a clear message. Make your closing remarks the same and you will leave your audience in style. They will respect you and admire your speaking ability. Most importantly, you will be successful in achieving your goal to be a persuasive speaker!

Below is a sample outline using the pyramid formula. Use it as a reference for your outlines. Notice how, "Step 3. Select your statistics and facts" has been incorporated into my outline.

Automobile Air bags: Are They Worth the Cost?

Win their attention

"Doesn't $1,500.00 sound like too much money to install a nine inch airbag in your car? $1,500.00 is a lot of money! Don't draw any conclusions yet though. I want to talk to you today about this new safety feature and show you some of the benefits we all can have if they become standard in every car. I want to start out by explaining how these airbags work as electronic systems"

Choose 3 - 5 specific subject areas

A. How airbags work as electronic systems

* usually three or four sensors are installed in front left, middle, and the front right of your car.

* electrical wiring runs from each sensor back to your steering column where airbag is located.

* 15 - 18 mph impacts will explode bag.

* As of today, only front end impacts will cause airbag to explode.

* sensors fire electronic message to steering column bag and bag explodes from gas pellets.

* bag has holes built into it so as soon is it explodes it deflates, preventing suffocation.

Transition statement here: "Let me explain the various options for installing airbags."

B. Cost of installation

* $1,500.00 charged by Dealerships, but insurance companies cover under a collision policy.

*   Local body shops charge under $1,000.00, but be careful, only trained technicians should do it.

*   It's smart to have your bag checked every six months.

Transition statement here: "I want to talk now about the benefits of Airbags."

C. Safety features: airbags save lives

*   Statistics from Insurance Institute of America showing dramatic benefit of an airbag on preventing fatalities and reducing major injuries.

*   Lisa Roberts story.

Draw your conclusion

"Most good insurance companies will pay to have your airbag re-installed after it has exploded in a car accident. Lisa Roberts has already benefited from her bag. I want my kids to benefit too. I say we make airbags standard in all cars built in the USA. It is worth the cost."

Summary

This chapter was written to give you an easy-to-use outline to organize your presentations. If you review the pyramid formula, you will see that outline. Etch the four parts of this outline in your mind. Organize your next five speeches using this formula. After applying my outline a few times and acquiring some public speaking experience, you will be able to add your own techniques to improve your speaking power. Mastering my outline is like learning the fundamental moves to make a basketball shot, or the basic steps to pass a football. Let's quickly review these fundamentals.

The first step is to sit down at your desk and write a short opening that is witty and wins people's attention. This is your last chance to make a good first impression. The opening remarks must be relevant to the purpose of the talk. Your entire opening could be one meaningful question or one story or funny anecdote told with animation. You have to stimulate your audience's interest right away.

The second step is to decide which three to five specific subjects you will talk about. You break down your general subject into specific subjects. Your audience's needs dictate what you will talk about. What do they want and need to hear? How will it benefit them? Choose subjects that are important not to you, but to your audience.

A brief comment here: Use transition statements! You know why! Audiences like organized talks.

The third step is choosing which statistics and facts to use. One statistic could really drive home a point, while seven statistics might confuse everybody. Common sense and good judgment are needed to make a wise decision. Do your homework. Prepare. Be able to defend your numbers. Distinguish fact from opinion. If you research your subject thoroughly, you will earn the respect of everyone.

The fourth and final step is to draw the conclusion. Tell your audience why your position is the best one for them to take. Summarize for them the key points and ask them if they have any questions. Ask them boldly to do something! Your goal is to get results. If you are selling something, ask for their business. If you are leading a cause ask them for their support in dollars or votes. People look for a message at the end of a movie, play, book, or one of your presentations. Send them a clear message and sit down!

That's it! You now have an easy outline to organize your presentations. My technique is very effective. It will work for any subject. You can use this outline for a seven-minute talk or a thirty-minute speech. Keep in mind your first few attempts at presentations will not be easy, but what in life worth pursuing is? Use my outline and you will become a persuasive speaker. Good luck!

SPEAKING YOUR BEST

Your checklist

☑ Win their attention

☑ Ask a smart question

☑ Tell a story

☑ Tell an anecdote

☑ Choose 3-5 meaningful subject areas

☑ Transition statements

☑ Select your statistics and facts

☑ Draw your conclusion

☑ Sample Outline

Chapter 2

Beating a ghost called fear

Does fear keep you from delivering effective presentations? If it does, you are not alone. Most people are afraid to stand up before a group and say more than their name and occupation. The first step toward developing better presentation skills is overcoming your fear.

What is it that you are afraid of? The most common fears people tell me about are the following. "I'm worried that I won't be able to speak with self confidence". "I would probably freeze up." "What if I don't have anything to say?" "I'm just not a bright person." "I would be a nervous wreck." "What if I make a mistake in front of everyone?" Do any of these hit a nerve with you? All of these fears are understandable. And all of them are easy to overcome. Let me show you how!

The best way to overcome public speaking fear is to understand it. Understand this then: your fear of talking before groups is more painful than talking before groups. As a member of a public speaking organization called Toastmasters International, I have watched many people give presentations. They all share one experience in common. Their fear deserts them after they start talking. The anxiety you feel prior to delivering a presentation is entirely created in your mind. Anything you can create in your mind you can also make go away. The hardest part of speaking before groups is not actually giving your talk. Once you start talking you'll do fine, and you will get even better with practice. It is this ghost called fear that makes you worry. You can eliminate this fear by understanding that it is you who controls this ghost. You have the power to make it disappear or let it keep you from being successful. This ghost called fear is harmless. Asking a few questions will help us see this phantom problem is easy to overcome.

Is the world going to come to an end if you make a mental or verbal slip while talking? No! Are you going to die in the middle of your presentation? No! Will you suddenly be exposed as a bad person once everyone sees you up in front? No! Will your career be made or broken in one presentation? No! What is the worse thing that can happen when you deliver a talk? Answer: you might perspire!

Speaking before a group of people is a lot of fun! It's a challenge, and like all challenges, giving a presentation is good for you. You will be forced to think when you deliver a talk, and this is good for you. You will have to express yourself, speak loudly, and show some emotion. This too, is good for you. In fact, you will feel great while you are talking. The adrenalin will be flowing throughout your body. It will feel like electricity is being generated inside you. Most people I meet like giving talks once they deliver their first one. They realize that the fear ghost is only in their heads.

Don't worry about making mistakes either! You will make them. I do. Everybody does! It's difficult to speak before a group, and your audience knows this. They expect you to make a few verbal slips now and then. Watch and listen to your television newscaster after work tonight. I guarantee you'll catch a few mispronounced words, or some *"uhs,"* and other verbal mistakes, and these media people get paid megabucks. There is no such thing as a slipless verbal speaker (unless they're naked). Make mistakes and live and learn.

The fact that fear is something you can control and eliminate is clearly demonstrated by refering to your nearest dictionary. The American Heritage dictionary defines the word fear as, "a feeling of alarm or disquiet caused by the expectation of danger, pain, disaster, or the like; terror, dread, apprehension." Note the word, "expectation" is key to the definition of fear. If you are walking in a forest and you hear a loud, aggressive growl, then your expectation that an animal is close by is real. You have good reason to be fearful. But to date I haven't heard of one speaker getting attacked by a wild animal while talking to an audience. In short, there is nothing <u>real</u> to be afraid of!

Now, do you understand this fictional ghost called fear? It really exists in your head. This means you can make it go away by simply understanding it. Fear holds people back from doing a lot of things in life that are worthwhile. But when you realize that performing the actual task is not nearly as tough as, "thinking about doing it," then you have taken a giant step forward. Here's another example of the ghost named fear.

I've been running three times a week for years. Running is fun, easy to do, and it relieves stress for me. I always run after work on the weekdays. To this day, I never feel like running before I actually run. After putting in eight hours on the job my body is *tired.* My mind is *tired.* So when I'm commuting home and I think about running, my mind says, "don't do it, you're too tired, worn out, exhausted. You've had a long, problem-filled day. Take a break, Kevin, and sit on the couch and watch some T.V." Another thought my mind conjures up is this: "Stop off and pick up some ice cream, go home and eat it. You deserve it."

These procrastinating thoughts always enter my mind prior to my going for a run. Since I create these fearful thoughts only I can get rid of them. How do I continue to run three times a week for years? It's easy! I use the same method I do to feel self confident before every presentation that I deliver. I just do it! I take control of my thoughts. I put on my running shoes and I run. When I'm about to deliver a presentation, I forget about my fears. The actual run or my presentation is easy once I start it. The only hard part is thinking about it. Overcoming the fear and finding the motivation is my goal. I understand this and turn off my fear. I don't listen to any negative thoughts that try to creep in. I turn them off like a leaky faucet and I just do it.

Do you recognize the advice that I am giving you? It's not some trendy psychological concept that's in fashion. It is called will power and self control. It is what your parents taught you when you were young. It is advice that means your success or failure depends not on some course, book, or something external. The power to change is within you. Benjamin Franklin made it his lifelong goal to practice self control and overcome the common fears that afflicted so many of the men and women of his day. The result was a man who played a big role in American History.

Mr. Franklin wasn't born with a high I.Q. He worked on improving his mind day after day. He realized that the power to control his thoughts with direction and purpose was within his control.

Summary

Forget about your fears! Spread you wings and go for it! If you are a manager or supervisor, throw any fearful thoughts out of your mind and give a motivational talk to your people. Deliver a persuasive presentation and tell your staff you'll be expecting 110% from them. Communication skills can shoot you to the top of your company or keep you on the lower rungs. Turn off your fears like a leaky faucet and give a dynamic presentation the next time you are at bat. You only have one life to live. Make the most of it! *Just do it!*

Your Checklist

☑ Beating a ghost called fear

Chapter 3

Good speakers apply these acting skills

Persuasive body language

It is a well known belief among veteran business people that body language and voice tone represent about 75% of persuasive communication. Only 25% is the actual words you use. This fact tells you that people are more influenced by how you say something than what you say. Your body's posture and your facial expression tell people a lot about you. Qualities like your self confidence, how happy you feel, and your physical health are examples of what people see when they look at you. Do you think these factors are important to the success of your presentation? You can bank on it!

This chapter benefits you by highlighting which acting skills good speakers apply. Reading it will increase awareness of your own body language and how to improve it. Glance through this chapter and make sure that you are presenting your talks with a persuasive personal style. Identify in which areas you need improvement and work on them. I guarantee you will get better if you do.

Eye contact

Establishing firm eye contact is very important when speaking to one person or to a group of people. When giving a talk to an audience of fifteen people or less you must look at each individual. You never want to make the audience feel like you are talking to only one person. Show respect by addressing everyone present.

My rule of thumb is that if you are speaking to fifteen people or less it's a good idea to look at each person at least *once* during a ten minute talk. If you speak longer than ten minutes, you must continue to address each person. The key point is to make sure you talk to everyone. Looking at each person demonstrates on a nonverbal level that you care about them.

The rules change if you're speaking to larger groups. It is too difficult to move from one person to another when you are speaking before crowds of twenty to one hundred people. My advice for groups this big is move your head and body to the left, turn to the middle, and then turn to the right. Alternate among these three positions during your speech, and the whole audience will feel like you are talking to them.

My experience in business tells me that most of the time you will be making presentations to small groups of people. How long should you look at each person? If you only glance at each individual they will still feel like you don't care about them. I'm effective when I look at each person for five seconds, then move on to the next person. This period of time shows each individual that you care enough to speak directly to them. Your nonverbal message is: I *respect* each one of you. Establishing good eye contact with your audience is the first acting skill a good speaker applies. You must do it to be persuasive.

Gestures

Why gesture? Because gestures add vitality, drama, and entertainment to your presentation. You can gesture with your arms, your hands, your fingers, your feet, and your whole body. You can paint a picture in your listener's minds with gestures. Gestures bring more value to your presentation. How do you gesture correctly? Read on!

Be natural and spontaneous in your gestures. Gestures must reflect the specific thought you are expressing. For example, if you say, "There are two reasons why your company needs the expertise of our consulting firm," that is when you can gesture by holding two fingers up. Use your common sense and you will gesture well.

Don't worry too much about using gestures every time you speak. They will come naturally. The one thing you don't want to do is gesture poorly. Here are some examples of poor gestures:

> keeping your hands in your pockets
> flailing your arms around like a madman
> pacing uncontrollably
> hanging your head down like a houndog
> playing with your hair
> slouching
> turning your back to your audience
> covering your mouth with your hand
> resting one foot on top of a chair
> sticking your finger in your ear (some people still do)

That's a big list. Avoid these poor gestures like *dandruff.* Review the following list of good gestures and be aware of when to use them. Use any one that you feel comfortable with.

Body erect and squarely facing the audience: This posture works best when you are covering the serious part of your speech and you want to show confidence. When you are defending your company, your products, or your ideas you should always be in this position. It is a good idea to start your talk with this posture. When you stand tall and squarely face the audience you project self confidence. Never slouch!

Clenched fist(s): This gesture shows power. It says to the audience, "I am a fighter." Military leaders often use this gesture. This was the national gesture of the black power movement in the 1960's. Since this gesture is a very aggressive one, you should invoke it with extreme caution. Use it only when your company or your job is on the line and want to broadcast to everyone that you are a fighter.

Open palm(s): This gesture is the symbolic gesture of giving. Jesus Christ is often pictured this way. If you're a minister, this gesture can be invoked during the offertory part of your services. When you're trying to bring fighting factions together you could try this gesture too.

Forefinger pointing toward the ceiling: This gesture means listen closely to what I am saying. The best moment to evoke this gesture is at the end of your presentation when you are summarizing your key points. Let's say it is the end of your sales presentation and your spoken words are, "Remember, I can save you time, money, and offer you years of reliable service." Now is when your forefinger can be brought into action.

Arms folded across your chest: This position projects strength and self discipline. The best time to use this gesture is when you are chatting afterwards with individual members in the room. This posture is a conservative one. Use it when engaged in casual conversation with business associates. One caveat: don't remain in this posture too long. You will very often find yourself stuck in one thought if you don't move out of this position within a minute or two. In a room full of people you can better influence more than one person if you keep moving and contacting the key players.

Hands clasped together in front of your chest: This gesture represents unity to those watching. It signals that you want your people to work together. Use it when some of your top players are having personality clashes. The best phrases to speak when using this gesture are, "we need to come together, or join sides, or work together, or work as a team."

Facial Expression

People form an impression of your attitude based on your facial expressions. It is important to send them the right message. Successful people have one thing in common: they project a positive self image. You, too, must project self confidence and show poise to get ahead in life. Your face can help you influence people effectively if it is full of expression.

When people look at you, they are looking to see if you are sad, happy, angry, frustrated, nervous, excited, bored, interested, relaxed, tired, aggressive, wimpy, uncertain, confident, dead or alive. Your face can project a great variety of emotions. Let me give you an example.

Suppose your boss says, "Bill, I want see you in my office immediately." If he is frowning or looks sad, you will feel nervous. If your boss is smiling or looks content, you will feel good. His facial expression affected your emotions.

There are an infinite number of facial expressions you can show to add emphasis to what you are saying. The key to success with facial expressions is using them consciously at the right moment in your talk. When you want your audience to feel sad, show them a frowning face. When you want to show enthusiasm, grin. If you want to show doubt, knit your eyebrows. Show them happiness by smiling for five seconds! How do you show them conviction? Stare *boldly* into their eyes without flinching.

Voice

Your voice, like your face, is a mirror of your heart. Your voice reflects how you feel about yourself. When you are self confident and happy, your voice will show it. When you are sad, or nervous, your voice reflects these emotions too.

How do you feel about someone who constantly speaks in a monotone? If you are like me, you feel anxious to escape this person's attention. How do you feel about someone who speaks in a high-pitched whine? If you're like most people, you lose respect for them. I've worked with a few MBA's in my career who knew a lot. But they never went far in the company because their voice, combined with their facial expression, revealed an insecure being was in our presence. I'm sorry, I'm frightened, I'm confused. These are nonverbal messages that a weak voice broadcasts. People judge you by the sound of your voice. Read this section carefully, take the voice test at the end of this chapter and learn the secrets to acquiring a winning voice.

Below is a brief description of the four components of a good speaking voice. *Study* them well.

Volume

When you speak, your voice must be loud enough so that everyone who is listening can hear you. It shouldn't be booming so that it shatters your listener's ear drums. It shouldn't be so quiet that people have to sit up and struggle to hear you. We all have a tendency to speak loudly when we are excited and quietly when we are bored. Most people speak too softly. Listen to yourself critically, ask good friends what they hear when you talk to them. Use the feedback to find the best volume for you. When you give a business presentation, you can spend the first minute adjusting your volume to fit the size of the room. Remember to speak <u>loudly</u> in a large room. A smart question to ask your listeners at the beginning of your talk is: *"Can everyone hear me?"* Believe it or not, many people don't ask this question and speak so quietly that some people can not hear them. A good tip is to speak to the farthest person away from you. If this person can hear you, everyone else can too.

Speed

How fast must you speak? Fast enough so that people have to pay attention to keep up with you, but slow enough to let them digest your message. If you are a high pressure type, you probably speak too quickly. Slow down a little! If your friends describe you as easygoing, you'll probably want to speed up your delivery. Find a comfortable speed that your audience likes. Remember, talk for your listener's comfort, not yours. In the best presentations I've heard, the speaker moved along at a brisk pace.

Tone

Tone measures how high or low your voice reaches on the musical scale. Tone can reveal your emotional state to people. If you are nervous, the tone of your voice will tell people just that. If you are unhappy, your voice sends an unhappy message.

The tone of your unique voice should be pleasing to your listeners. It should reflect a mature individual. It shouldn't be gutteral or whiny. If you have good control over your emotions your tone should be fine. One technique is to listen to work associates, superiors, or friends who speak well and learn from them. With a little practice, you can easily learn to control your tone so people like listening to it. Most of the time your tone should be positive and upbeat.

Vocal variety

Vocal variety is important in your presentation because people like listening to an animated speaker. Vocal variety is achieved by varying the volume, speed, and tone of your voice. Like an actor, your voice should reflect a wide range of emotions. Let your voice broadcast to your listeners happiness, anger, sincerity, commitment, suspicion, and hope.

The best advice to learn how to add variety to your voice is to listen to radio or T.V. broadcasters. Listen to how clearly they speak and how much variety they display in telling you about local politics or another auto accident. Vocal variety is an essential skill good speakers demonstrate. You will be surprised how interested people become in what you're saying when you say it with vocal variety. You can add it to your speaking style and become a more *persuasive* speaker.

Voice test

Turn on a cassette tape player and record your own speaking voice. Pick up a newspaper or book and read it for five minutes. Now playback your talk. How does your voice sound to you? Is it an interesting, thought provoking voice? Does your voice sound happy, sad, tired, bored, animated or lively?

Is there vocal variety in it? Is it monotone? Would you like listening to this person speak for twenty minutes? This method of voice improvement is easy and it doesn't cost anything, yet it can change a poor or average speaker into a dynamic one. I know, because I have used it and subsequently received many kudos for a *"dynamic presentation."* Listen to your voice on the tape player and correct any bad habits. It's one of the tools smart actors use.

Summary

This chapter has focused entirely on delivery style. How you say something is equally as important as what you say. If you take two salespeople or two job applicants or two employees interviewing for a promotion, the one who presents himself, or herself, with more poise and self confidence will win. Competition for promotions and jobs is keen in America today. You need every edge you can get. Study the body language skills illustrated in this chapter. Reflect on your own style. Is it persuasive? Identify your bad speaking habits - everybody has a few - and eliminate them. Show self confidence in your next presentation by looking at people in their eyes for five seconds. Focus your eye contact on the people you want to influence the most. Gesture with your hands in a bold manner to drive home an important point. Be expressive with your whole body. Develop a mature speaking voice. Add vocal variety to your next talk. Speak with enthusiasm and conviction. Display positive nonverbal body language. You will be a more persuasive speaker and influence people greater if you practice these habits. These are the acting skills good speakers apply. *Good Luck!*

Checklist

☑ Persuasive body language

☑ Eye contact

☑ Gestures

☑ Facial expression

☑ Voice

☑ Volume

☑ Speed

☑ Tone

☑ Vocal variety

☑ Voice test

Chapter 4

The secret to opening and closing your talks

The two parts of a presentation that impact people the most are the open and the close. This book would not be complete if I didn't show you how to master these two areas. Many intelligent people make costly mistakes when they start and finish their talks because they do not know how to do it right. After you read this chapter you'll understand the secret to opening and closing your presentations like a professional speaker. It is easy to deliver a good open and close when you apply these techniques.

The Open

Why is the beginning of your presentation critical? Because you never get a second chance to make a good first impression! Believe it or not, people remember only about 25% of what you tell them, and most of what they recall will be from your opening. The first two minutes are when everyone judges you. People will stare at you and ask themselves, "Is he bright?" "Is she experienced?," "Did he prepare for this talk?" Is she organized?" "Am I bored already with this guy?" "Does she know what she's doing?"

Your opening must be memorable to be effective. It has to grab the attention of your audience like a red light stops motorists. The best openings are funny. And by funny I don't mean slapstick funny, I mean witty. Most of the people you'll be speaking to will be educated and informed adults. You want to earn their respect as a leader and their affinity as a human being. A humorous opening that ties into the main message of your presentation will warm up your audience quickly.

Memorize your opening remarks

How do you give a good opening? The first tip is to memorize every word of your opening. If you are asked to speak without notice, this is obviously impossible, but for a prepared talk, it is a good idea. Your opening might be one sentence or it might be five, but you have to know it by heart. When you know your opening cold, you will be able to show self confidence and make a good first impression. Now you can focus on your delivery technique. You can look everyone in the eye and establish rapport right away. You won't have to think about what you are saying and it will sound very natural. The first few moments are the most difficult for all speakers, and by knowing your opening like the skin on your nose, you'll be off to a good start. Here is an example:

I gave a talk in 1991 on the subject of No Fault insurance in California. At the time I was an adjuster for a major insurance company and I watched many unscrupulous individuals cheat my company by making fraudulent claims. The purpose of my presentation was to arouse anger in the audience toward these people so they would vote yes on No Fault. I felt strongly that No Fault would prevent these con artists from stealing money and causing everyone's car insurance premiums to rise. Under No Fault law you can't sue the insurance company of the person that hit you, unless you were seriously hurt. Every insurance company had to offer full medical coverage to all policy holders. This way everyone is protected and it eliminates the profit incentive for making phony injury claims. The body of my presentation contained statistics and facts supporting my argument but I knew this would be boring for some people. I needed to open with a lot of emotional *punch* to grab everyone's attention. My opening turned out to be a winner. I memorized it so I could look at everyone and focus on my emotional delivery. Here's what I said:

"Good evening everyone. (3 second pause.) I work as an auto insurance adjuster in California, and, to be honest with you people, I am a *"very angry adjuster."* I'm angry because..."

My opening was met with smiles and laughter. Everyone was curious to know who and what I was angry about. I won their attention fast. Do you know why this opening worked for me? Because I was able to connect with the audience on an emotional or gut level. Everyone gets angry! We all get mad throughout each day at one thing or another. Anger is a big part of life. I also showed them that I was a person who felt things just like them. I said, "Hey, I'm Kevin Boland, I'm an angry man, and I'm here to tell you why." The rest of my talk would be full of cold statistics and facts supporting my argument, but my opening was full of emotion, and they wouldn't forget it.

Here are ten examples of good openings. Some of these can be used for a variety of talks, but I recommend you always write your own opening to make it unique and keep it *fresh*.

Sample Openings

1. "I can feel the excitement in the air tonight, and I'm proud to be a part of it."

2. "I was asked to share with you tonight my proven methods of losing weight. My first tip is give a lot of talks, because you'll be so nervous you'll sweat off pounds."

3. "Tonight we have to make a decision about who we are going to hire for our next Vice-President, let's keep in mind the best person for the job might not be the most popular, but he or she must be the one who earns our respect."

4. "I gathered you department heads here because we have to fire some of your staff, I don't like it at all, but it has to be done, and I want you to do it intelligently and with compassion for those who have to go."

5. "Tonight I will speak to you about a subject that can kill you: cigarette smoking."

6 ."How many people in the room think one million dollars is a lot of money? Well, that's how much new business we lost last quarter because our x product isn't selling!"

7 ."We saved a lot of money last year thanks to our new cost control policy, and as a result, the future of our organization looks bright!"

8. "There are three things I want to say to your salespeople today: sell, sell, sell!"

9. Living the Christian life can be very difficult sometimes, but then again, that's why devout Christians are known as soldiers of Christ. Today's sermon will explore ways in which we

Christians can build our spiritual strength, so each day we can be ready for the good battle."

10. "It's easy to point our fingers at this big oil company and blame it for the destruction of the environment, but don't we all benefit by driving our cars, heating our homes, and don't we all enjoy a standard of living unparalleled in the world? I'm pointing my finger at this company and praising it, and you should too."

I hope these examples of good openings help you understand the common technique they all use. Each one shoots straight for the heart of the audience. Each opening is emotional. The body of your presentation will contain the cold facts and statistics supporting your argument. Begin your talks with a little drama and the results will surprise you. All of these openings were well thought out and tie into the central theme of the speaker's talk too. Do you notice that every opening uses direct, straight from the hip language? Don't think people are impressed with your big vocabulary; they'll respect you more for your wisdom than how many big words you know. Start getting into the habit of being direct with people. Nobody likes a windbag. Jump start your presentations with emotional punch. The first habit a good speaker practices is a strong opening. You must do the same to be persuasive.

The Close

There are two elements you must include in your close to be effective: a clear message and emotional punch! This is true because at the end of your talk people will ask themselves,

"What's the message?" People look for meaning at the end of a story, a movie, a book, or a presentation. Your closing remarks must deliver a clear message!

The second vital element in your close is emotional punch. Just like your openings, you must close out your talks with a little drama. Many speakers give organized talks and then deliver an emotionless close. This costly mistake weakens an otherwise solid presentation. When I suggest that you close with emotion I'm not implying you should act like a melancholy boob. I am advising you to use the sensible emotion that is appropriate. If your presentation was lighthearted and humorous, than your close should be the same. If you talked about sin and it's destructive effects, you might want to end on a somber note. If you're asking people to donate time or money for a charitable cause, you will need to show compassion. People remember information presented to them better if the speaker is animated. Your close is your last chance to score points with your listeners. Deliver a clear *message* and say it with *emotion.*

Here are ten examples of good closes. Use these as frames of reference whenever you write your own concluding remarks. Examine them carefully and you will see they contain the two elements of all effective closes: a clear *message* and emotional *punch.*

Sample Closings

1. "The Senator's record on abortion speaks for itself: terrible!"

2. "In closing, I want to beat up everyone in the market in three areas: price, service and quality."

3. "An old saying my dad was fond of repeating to me is charity begins at home." I feel today that some editing of this useful phrase is needed. "In our church, charity begins at home, but ends only *after* all our members' needs are met."

4. "I began my talk today by describing how well we did this year in eating away at our competitor's market share. I'll finish it by telling you that I'm still very hungry for more market share next year."

5. "This afternoon you men will be playing for the 1975 High School football championship of Philadelphia. There's only two ways you'll leave the stadium today, winners or losers. Which will it be?"

6. "What strikes me most clearly about the prosecution's case is the lack of one piece of solid evidence proving beyond a reasonable doubt that my client, Pat Brady, committed any crime. No, ladies and gentlemen of the jury, no proof exists. None! There is a criminal out there who embezzled funds, and I want the police to catch him too, but that person isn't Pat Brady."

7. "The next time a prospect asks you for information about our products, respond quickly and thank them for their interest. If you do, you'll see some of them again as clients."

8. "Performance standards were designed to be adjusted only one way people: Up!"

9. "A positive attitude does more than make you feel good about yourself. It makes other people feel good about you too, and when they do, they buy your product."

10. "What do you get when one Democrat works with one Republican: an efficient government."

Summary

Don't overlook the importance of memorizing your opening remarks. If you know your opening, you can focus on your delivery style and make a good first impression. The first two minutes are critical. People will be judging you. Act self confident and open with emotion and a little drama. Establish good eye contact right away. Write a witty opening that's memorable.

The close demands equal attention from you. People expect something meaningful at the end of your talk. Don't disappoint them. The close is when you ask for the order. The close is for summarizing the purpose of your presentation. Close with enthusiasm. Deliver a clear message. Show some guts and be emotional. As long as your feelings are appropriate, people will respect you for your courage.

Remember: the two parts of your presentation people remember the most are the open and the close. Don't ruin an otherwise solid presentation by opening or closing weakly. Apply the advice given in this chapter and you'll be more *persuasive* in your presentations. Good luck!

Checklist

☑ The Open

☑ Memorize your Opening Remarks

☑ Sample Openings

☑ The Close

☑ Sample Closings

Chapter 5

Speaking off-the-cuff

My worst memory of speaking before a group of people was during my junior year in college. I signed up for a course in rhetoric, and on the first day, the teacher said he wanted us to say a few words about ourselves. I was unlucky since I had to go first because my last name began with a "B."

Our teacher was a big guy with a booming voice. He shouted out, "Mr. Boland, you're first!" As soon as I stood up, fear grabbed me. My mouth felt like a jar of peanut butter. To this day, I can't recall what I said. All I remember is sprinting for my chair afterwards. Has this ever happened to you?

Fortunately, I survived my first test in speaking off-the-cuff, but it left me with a healthy respect for any person with the self confidence to speak well before a group. My experience also motivated me - fear always motivates - to become effective at impromptu speaking. You can learn how to do it too! It's a lot easier when you use proven techniques. In the next few pages I'll give you the secrets to be an effective off-the-cuff speaker. And admit it, isn't speaking with short notice the way it usually happens in the real world? Let me prepare you for your next off-the-cuff talk by relying upon proven techniques.

Nine techniques to use

Be ready

This obvious suggestion is often ignored by many people. If you are a staff person in your organization your manager may do all the talking at each week's meeting, but one of these days don't get caught brain dead if he asks you to say something. And if you are a manager, and you get an invitation to another department's meeting, be ready to answer a question or make an insightful suggestion. Snooze and you loose! Always be thinking and anticipating what's on the agenda and what someone might ask you to say. If you're expected to be there, be there mentally. Be ready!

<u>Pause</u>

The first thing to do when you're asked suddenly to speak is pause. Take five or ten seconds to collect your thoughts. This tip sounds easy but most people panic as soon as they hear their name. They start talking without thinking and don't say anything worthwhile. You don't want to rush right into your answer. Because this is an impromptu talk, you need the five to ten seconds to formulate an intelligent response. By applying this tip and pausing, you'll be amazed at the results. People will be impressed with your poise for taking a moment to collect your thoughts. This technique works everyday in business too. If your manager or co-worker asks you a question, don't rush into an answer. Force yourself to stop and think! I guarantee your answer will be better when you pause before replying.

Speak slowly: it helps you relax

This third tip is very important: speak slowly and relax. I'll bet you're thinking that is easy for me to say. I know that you are going to get nervous before every talk you deliver. But what I'm suggesting is that you control the nervousness. When you pause in the beginning you give yourself time to start off intelligently. By speaking slowly throughout your talk you're controlling your fear and this helps you relax. Think about it! Whenever you deliberately slow down and speak to anyone you relax yourself. Don't panic just because there are a few people listening to you. Slow down and relax. Let's discuss one more benefit to speaking slowly.

You don't have time to prepare for off-the-cuff talks. When you are on the spot, you need to take time to think carefully about what you're saying. By speaking slowly you give your mind time to think while you're speaking. As you speak slowly, you'll gain insights. You will be able to analyze what you say as you say it. Your mind works ten times faster than your voice; slowing down lets your brain work comfortably ahead of your voice. Speaking slowly will help you relax and think on your feet intelligently.

Less is More

This fourth tip is my favorite: less is more. What does this mean? The most common mistake people make in impromptu speaking is talking too much. They ramble on and on without saying anything meaningful. Be specific in your reply. Say something intelligent and sit down. Don't try to take on your entire company's problems in a couple of minutes. Whatever the question or issue thrown at you, get to your specific thoughts on the subject and conclude.

Be enthusiastic

A lot of people let themselves become bored when listening to others speak. All of a sudden they're called upon to talk and they sound sleepy. Pay attention at all times! In business, you can never afford to be caught napping. When someone asks you to say a few words, stand up and look lively! Even if you don't have anything new to say, say it with enthusiasm. At least you will score points for being energetic.

Use humor

A witty comment that is not offensive will score points for you. If you can say something intelligent and funny, you will win a few friends. People love to laugh because it relieves stress. Be careful to always use appropriate humor. If you can not think of anything profound to say, a good witticism will endear you to the audience.

Never apologize

Never apologize for not being prepared. The rest of the group should know you didn't have time to prepare. If they don't, tell them you were asked to speak without notice, you can say something like, "I was asked to fill in for Bob because his flight was delayed at O'Haire Airport. I haven't had a chance to review last month's figures because of the short notice, but I can give you an overview of the first quarter's results. " Remember, you never want to put yourself in a position of apologizing because it makes you look weak. And if you do not have a lot to say on the subject under discussion, don't say "I'm sorry, that's about all I can think of..." That statement may be true, but it also tells everyone that you are uninformed. It also makes you look weak. Instead, if you don't have anything to say, try this approach, "I've been immersed in working on the new sales promotion this week, I haven't had time to read that report."

Can you see how the second approach is more positive for you? Do not assume people at the meeting will excuse your ignorance on a subject. They won't. They'll assume you were briefed but think you are dull unless you choose your words carefully. Never apologize.

Speak loudly

Sound silly? Think again. Speaking loudly does a couple of things for you. First, when you turn up the volume in your voice it wakes you up. It can snap you out of a daydream. Second, other people will pay attention to you more. They may not agree with what you're saying, but they will be impressed that you are bold enough to say it loudly. Remember the old saying, "the squeaky wheel gets the grease." It's true. Obviously, common sense applies here. You can't speak so loud that it turns people off. But think of the people you work with. I'll bet you $5.00 there are some mice in the group. People who are insecure speak quietly because they hope that by doing so, the world will ignore them, and they are *right.* If you want to be overlooked for that next promotion, speak quietly. If you want to be noticed, speak loudly.

Show self confidence

Life is a game. The people who play it smart and win, play it with self confidence. When you are called upon to speak, stand up or sit up in your chair. Hold you head up high and keep your eyes facing forward. Body language can either help you or hurt you. Droopy shoulders and eyes looking down tell people you are shy and weak. Square shoulders and eyes forward tells them you have poise and know where you're going. Show self confidence in your voice too. Speaking slowly and choosing your words wisely earns the respect of others. Even if you are asked only to give your name and why you are there, say it with self confidence. When you act self confident something amazing happens: *people believe you!*

Summary

Impromptu speaking is difficult. It's hard because you don't have time to prepare. The nine techniques for speaking off-the-cuff presented in this chapter work. I use them Monday through Friday in my company. They will work for you too! The next time you hear your name called out to say a few words, pause a couple of seconds and collect your thoughts. You will surprise yourself by making an intelligent suggestion with *confidence.* Good luck!

Your checklist

☑ Be ready

☑ Pause

☑ Speak slowly: it helps you relax

☑ Less is more

☑ Be enthusiastic

☑ Use humor

☑ Never apologize

☑ Speak loudly

☑ Show self confidence

Chapter 6

How to use visual aids

T here is one compelling reason why visual aids are effective and it's a simple one: people like pictures. They learn better using them. A wise Irishman once said, "Tell someone something and they'll probably forget it. Show them something, and they'll remember it a long time." Good visual aids add promotional *punch* to your presentation. They often make the logical flow of ideas easier to comprehend. A good visual aid can simplify a lot of statistical information. A pie chart can break down an entire organization's sales, marketing, finance and manufacturing costs. You can be creative too, and use a unique visual aid to help you sell. Here's an example.

When I was selling fax machines in California, I made a lot of money using visual aids that you have in your possession right now. Curious? Pull out your wallet or purse. My visual aid is in your hand! Here's what I did: I would figure out how much *money* I could save a company using my plain paper fax machine. My plain paper fax used regular photocopy paper, which was less expensive than typical thermal fax paper. I still had objections to overcome though. Very few sales are easy and my machine cost more than normal fax machines.

My visual aid helped me close quite a few sales. What was it? I'd deposit in front of them $355.39 of real *money* if that was their monthly savings. My visual aid always sat there during the rest of my presentation so they could see it. I got a lot of sales using this visual and many of my clients would tell me later, "Kevin, your idea to leave all that real money on our desk was unique. It showed us clearly how much money we were spending on that slippery thermal paper that nobody likes anyway."

If you have to give information to a group of people in a short period of time (and what successful person doesn't?), then you need to learn how to use visual aids effectively. My example of using real money demonstrates that you can choose a unique visual to get your point across. Most of the time though, you will be using the traditional visual aids described below. Lets examine them.

The Flip Chart

The most common visual aid in corporate offices today is the flipchart. The flipchart is inexpensive and easy to use. Here are some tips to keep in mind when working with them.

Don't speak while facing the flipchart with your back to the audience. Face the group and talk because some people won't be able to hear you, and others will feel offended when you turn your back on them. Avoid standing in any position where you might block someone's vision. Write in large letters and write neatly. If you received a "D" in elementary school for pennmanship, be extra careful to print legibly.

Choose your words carefully on each flipchart page. Underline your key points. Don't write long sentences. Use short and concise words. Use ***bullet*** points to highlight the features or benefits of your product.

Be sure to organize your ideas in the right time sequence. For example, page one must be your opening, page two your next idea and so on. When you finish discussing something on one of your flipchart pages and start a new subject, turn the page so nobody is still looking at an old subject. It's a good idea to use two or three different colored pens to separate subjects. This helps for *clarity*. You must also bring a pointer with you for your presentation. I guarantee you will look more professional using this handy tool to highlight information on your flipchart.

You must use a flipchart only when your audience is small enough so that every person can see it. Fifteen feet is about as far away as anyone can see your printed information. Keep this in mind when setting up. Finally, make sure you have plenty of pages left on your flipchart so you don't find yourself frantically running out at the last minute to buy some more. The flipchart is an effective tool. You can purchase one for under $75.00. Buy one and use it if you are giving talks to groups of fifteen people or less.

The Overhead Projector

The overhead projector is another tool that is easy to operate and helps you present information easily. Here are some tips on using one.

The projector is a smart choice of visual tools when you have a lot of information to cover in your presentation. You can write down more information on one page of a transparency than you can on a few flipchart pages. The second benefit of the projector is that you can deliver your presentation to a much larger audience than you can using a flipchart. It is possible to project your image onto a large screen so that a hundred people or more can see it.

A projector is easy-to-use. There is a plug, a power on and off button, and an adjustable fixture on top that allows you to focus your image on the screen. This fixture is just like the lens on a camera. You adjust it until the image is clear on the screen. All it takes is one time setting up your projector to become a pro at it.

When you give a talk with an overhead projector you will use what are called transparencies or acetates. These are 8 1/2 x 11 inch blank transparent pieces of plastic. You can write directly on them and your words and drawings will be projected onto the screen. You can purchase these transparencies at any local stationary supply store.

A lot of executives use personal computers to print out charts, bar graphs and typed text onto regular paper, then send these to a local copy store to have the information transferred to a transparency. It is also possible to print out transparencies using a personal computer. Simply insert the blank transparencies into your printer's receiving tray. This approach lets you project computer designed graphics onto your screen. This saves you time writing on your transparencies and the computer can print more legibly than most of us. You can always keep a few blank transparencies with you in case you want to write something new in the middle of your presentation too.

During your presentation remember to talk to your group, not to the projector. Always keep in mind that although the projector is a powerful visual tool, it is *you* and your analysis that the people came to hear. Don't expect the projector to do your selling for you. You must be an animated narrator who interprets what these pictures on the screen mean. It's a good idea to choose someone ahead of time to switch the lights off and on for you. Another good tip is to turn the projector off whenever you speak. Some projectors can be very noisy. Be certain also that you have an extension cord long enough to reach the wall socket.

Use common sense when setting up the projector. Place it toward the back of the room, in the middle, so everyone has a *clear view* of the screen. It's also a good idea to bring a pointer with you. Often there will be chairs, tables, or a bulky projector stand to get in your way of highlighting some statistic on your screen. Using a pointer will allow you to reach over these obstacles. Another good tip is to number your transparencies so that you won't get them out of order. Imagine how foolish you will look if right in the middle of your talk, you are suddenly groping for a missing page. There goes your big raise!

One final caveat about using the overhead projector: always bring a spare bulb with you. I have seen bulbs burn out in the middle of presentations. The bulb burns out when in use only, so avoid embarrassment and pack a spare one.

The Slide Projector and VCR

The two other visual aids you will see sometimes are the slide projector and the VCR. Both of these aids are easy to operate. I think it would be a waste of good paper and valuable ink to spend time talking about these two tools that are easy to use. Use your common sense and you'll do fine. The previous tips about using the flipchart and the overhead projector apply to these aids also. Just keep in mind that *you* are the *star* of the presentation, not the visual aid. Don't disappoint your audience. Give them a good show!

Summary

A good point about using visual aids in particular and giving presentations in general is that you must rehearse. I recommend running through a presentation twice before the real thing. This advice applies double when visual aids are going to play an important role in your presentation. Remember to never let your audience focus too long on your visual aid and not on you. It's your presentation! People came to hear you speak to them. Stay in control at all times and be animated!

Visual aid tools are easy to use and add entertainment value to your presentation. You have the option of using some unique visual to make a point or you can rely upon the traditional tools, or you can use a combination of both. Those old sayings like, "seeing is believing," and "a picture says a thousand words" are true. People remember something a lot longer when you show them in addition to just telling them. Follow my advice in this chapter and you won't experience any problems using visual aids. They will help you deliver a more professional presentation. Good Luck!

Your Checklist

☑ The flipchart

☑ The overhead projector

☑ The slide projector and VCR

Chapter 7

A fast and easy way to outline your talk

The five w's: who, what, when, where, and why

Sound familiar? The last time you heard this phrase was probably in high school. I have included this piece of advice for those managers who are so busy you rarely have time to sit down and outline a presentation. This method of organizing your talk is effective if your subject matter is concrete and you are giving people the facts. It's a great way to organize your weekly departmental meetings or when you are asked to speak on short notice. Journalists use this technique when they write short newspaper articles. Let me show you how it works.

WHO

Journalists use the, "who" part of their article to refer to whom they are writing about. When you give a presentation however, the "who" part means what type of people are listening to you. Here are some questions to ask before deciding what to say to them:

Who are the people you will be speaking to? What are their feelings toward your subject? Are they your superiors, employees, or co-workers? Are they salespeople or accountants? Business people or academics? Healthcare professionals or hospital administrators? Housewives or career women? Californians or New Yorkers? Young or old? New employees or veterans? Conservative or liberal? Rich, poor or the middleclass? City dwellers or country folk? Homeowners or tenants? Computer workers or insurance employees? Natives or foreigners? Executives or managers?

Why is it important to know who your audience is? Because you will use a *different approach* depending upon who you are presenting too. If you give a presentation to your superiors, you better show respect for their position and be sensitive not to take too much control of the meeting. On the other hand, if you're addressing your staff, you better take the role of the leader and maintain control. If you don't, your staff will lose respect for you.

If you are talking to computer people, use phrases like software bugs or peripheral equipment. If you are speaking to salespeople, use phrases like closing the sale, or setting up the prospect where appropriate. In addition, keep in mind that a salesperson's feeling toward a product will be different from a marketing person. The sales representative will think of the product in terms of it's features and benefits. The marketing person will think about the same product in terms of its price, availability, costs, and sales history. The marketing person will be less emotional toward the product and more analytical. The point of asking these questions is for you to understand your audience. Use common sense and think carefully about what type of people they are. It will help you write a custom outline for them.

WHAT

The second part is easy. What will you be talking about? What facts do you want to mention. Which statistics are worth highlighting? What specific subject categories are you going to talk about? Which issues, events, or problems will you decide are more important to discuss than others? The "what" part helps you choose the nuts and bolts of your presentation. Here, you limit yourself to certain subjects which you feel are high priority for this talk.

WHEN

What time of day will it be when you speak? Morning or afternoon? Before or after lunch? Monday or Friday? During regular business hours or at a local restaurant after work? How much time will you be alotted to speak? Will you be the first speaker or the last? These questions are useful. If you are speaking at 8 a.m. you'll want to start slowly to give people time to wake up. You might want to encourage people to get a cup of coffee before you start. If you're presenting on Friday afternoon tell your group that you know it's quitting time and you promise to keep it short. Be careful to keep a talk short if you are speaking before a meal. Audiences are rough on empty stomachs!

WHERE

Where is it that you will be speaking? The where part of your outline addresses logistical issues. Will you be talking in a hotel banquet room or an engineering lab? A conference room or an employee break room? This part helps you determine if you need a microphone or not. Will you need to speak loudly or should you be careful to talk quieter because the room will be small? Will there be unexpected interruptions? You may be talking in an employee lunch room, so be prepared if employees from other departments walk in to get a coke from the vending machine. This part helps you prepare for seating arrangements and handouts, lighting and visual aid displays. How long will it take you to get there? Do you need to have a custodian on hand to unlock the classroom? Will you be speaking from a podium? Will you be standing in front of, or in the center of, the group? From a stage or a level area? Don't overlook this part. Many a speaker has been stung by a communication breakdown and arrived at the *wrong* place to deliver a presentation.

WHY

The best has been saved for last. Why are your spending everyone's valuable time talking to them? What is the major objective of your presentation? Is it to sell something? Is it motivational? Educational? Are you going to browbeat your staff on last month's performance? Will you be selecting individual achievers for recognition? Do you want to let everyone know that you think they are doing a good job? Are there new procedures you need to explain? Are changes coming to the organization? Is this presentation a good opportunity for you to show off your intelligence to some top executives who will be in attendance? Is your major objective to get acceptance for a new computer system? If you are a new manager, do you want to put everyone on notice that you are tough and will be raising performance standards?

In every presentation that you deliver you must know clearly what your major objective is. Ambiguous goals give poor results. Why are you talking? What is it you want to accomplish? An easy technique I frequently use is to write down in one sentence what my major objective is. This <u>forces</u> me to think. It gives me self confidence going into a presentation when I know clearly why I am talking to everyone. For example, let's say I will be talking to my staff this week. My objective could be written this way. "My goal this week is to show my staff that I know how busy this month has been for them and that I really appreciate their efforts." Or how about this sentence, "My main purpose today is to give my employees the feeling that even though there have been some management changes, their jobs are <u>not</u> in jeopardy, and our future looks bright."

Summary

There are two circumstances that merit using the five W's approach: weekly meetings and speaking with only a few hours notice. It's a fast and easy way to organize your talk. It's a proven method that has rescued me on several occasions. It will help you organize your thoughts into logical categories. This is a unique method because it is easy to apply, yet thorough in forcing you to ask the right questions. Any weekly agenda can be organized under these five headings. Use it when you don't have much time to prepare. The five W's will help you stay organized and, consequently, persuasive. Good Luck!

SPEAKING YOUR BEST

Checklist

 Who

✔ What

✔ When

✔ Where

✔ Why

Chapter 8

How to present statistics

About half the speakers out there are competent in delivering their presentations, until they present statistics. It probably has something to do with the "Math fear" that many people feel. Whatever the reason, too many clear presentations are tarnished by a dull delivery of numbers. Like every other aspect of presentations, the ability to stun your audience with statistics is easy if you present them the correct way. Listen carefully to my advice. You don't have to be an MBA graduate to be effective at presenting statistics. All you need is the knowledge and the *desire* to use it.

What is statistics and how can it help you? Statistics is the collection, organization, and interpretation of data. Most people use this discipline to support their arguments and to measure activity in their business. Some analysts also extrapolate about the future based on historical data. This chapter will only scratch the surface about statistics. If you want to learn more about this field take a course or purchase a "Statistics Made Easy" book at a local bookstore. My goal in this chapter is to show you how to use some common statistical measures to bolster your presentation. I also want to stress that it's important to choose statistical facts wisely, and present them correctly. The biggest mistake made by people is choosing too much data, and then presenting it in such a way that it obfuscates the audience. Here are a few common statistical measures.

Arithmetic mean (average)

The term arithmetic mean is synonymous with average. The mean is the number obtained by dividing the sum of a set of quantities by the number of quantities in the set. For example, determine the sum of these quantities: 82, 84, 95, 93, 78. Answer: 432. Now divide the sum, "432," by the number of quantities in the set, "5." Answer: 86.4. The answer 86.4 is the arithmetic mean or average of all the numbers in the set. If these numbers represented scores for a national math test you could say that the average score among students was 86.4 *(incredible!)*. If you were one of the students, you could see how well you did compared to the average student.

Here is another way to use the average measure. Suppose you were the manager of five sales offices and you wanted a way to measure how well each office is doing. You could measure how well each office is doing compared to the company average. Using the same rule as above add up the total of your five sales territories. Oakland: $121,000.00 San Francisco: $123,000.00 San Rafael: $36,000.00 San Jose: $80,000.00 and Berkeley: $25,000.00 The sum is $385,000.00 The average territory sales volume in your company might be $133,000.00 Now, how are your territories doing compared to the company's average? Dividing the total sales of your offices by five gives you $77,000.00 The average sales volume for your territories is $77,000.00, well below the company average of $133,000.00 *You better look for another job!* Or, maybe you should take a close look at the Berkeley and San Rafael territories since they are your worst offices. You could also argue that Berkeley and San Rafael are smaller cities than San Francisco, Oakland and San Jose, and that's why sales are bad.

Do you see how you can use the arithmetic mean or average to present your data. Let's take a look at another statistical measure:

Percentage

Percentage means some part of the common denominator one hundred. When people speak about percentages they are telling you that some figure is part of a bigger number. For example, in our sales territory illustration above total sales are $385,000.00 Sales in the San Rafael territory are $36,000.00 If you divide $36,000 by $385,000.00 you get 9%. This computation tells you that the San Rafael territory is only generating 9% of total sales. In many companies today the percentage is the most frequently used statistical measure.

There are many ways you can use percentages. If you want to mark up the price of a product by 20% all you have to do is multiply the price you paid for it by .20. Let's say you buy candy and sell it in your grocery store. If the product costs you $2.00 multiply $2.00 by .20. Answer .40. Now add .40 to $2.00 and you get $2.40, which is a 20% mark up in price. What if you wanted to argue that there are more men in executive positions in a company than women? To support your contention find out how many executive positions exist in the company. Then find out how many women are in executive positions. Now divide the number of women in executive positions by the total number of executive positions. Example: 18 total executive jobs. Only 3 are occupied by females. 3 divided by 18 =.17 which can be stated as 17%. (to change a decimal into a percent simply move the decimal point over two places to the right.) Now you can boldly state that only 17% of the executive positions are filled by women.

Do you understand how to use percentages now? If not, just review the above examples and create some of your own until it becomes clear. Let's examine a third statistical measure.

Ratio

Ratios are easy to understand. In fact, we already used one. A ratio can be a number or a percentage that shows the relationship between two quantities. When we looked at our sales territories we saw that the five sales territories were averaging $77,000.00. If we compare the $77,000.00 to the amount of money generated by the average sales territory in the company, $133,000.00, we are looking at the relationship between the two figures. To state the relationship as a ratio we would to do this: $133,000.00:$77,000.00. To express this ratio in percentages we divide $77,000.00 by $133,000.00 which gives us .58. Now we can say that the five territories sales figures are 42% below the company average (.58 is .42 shy of 100). Another way we can express the ratio of the average five territories sales volume compared to the company's average is by stating this: "For every two dollars worth of business generated by the average company office only a little over one dollar is generated by your average territory's." We can say this because $133,000.00 is almost double $77,000.00. The ratio is almost 2:1.

How to present your numbers

Now you know three different ways to use statistics in your presentation: arithmetic mean (average), percentage and ratio. The next step is understanding the correct way to present them to your audience.

The key to success with statistics is applying a two step formula. The first step is deciding which figures are significant to your specific audience. The second step is presenting those numbers in *clear* language. Let's look at the first step.

Experienced business people know the importance of choosing the right numbers. Quality beats out quantity. You don't need ten statistical examples if one will get the job done. In order to decide which numbers to highlight you must look at your audience. Who will be there? Will you be speaking to students, housewives, senior citizens, vice-presidents, staff or factory workers? The people in your audience determine which numbers you will choose. For example, if you are talking to your salespeople, pick numbers that let them see how well they are doing selling certain products. You might also pick figures that show them which products they need to improve their volume on. On the other hand, if you are addressing the board of directors you should choose figures that highlight profit and loss areas, since boards are mainly concerned about the bottom line. Think about your audience and what they care about to discover which data to include in your presentation. The world is full of special interest groups. Choose figures that interest your specific group.

Politicians are inveterate experts at presenting statistics that cloud their rival's public service record. A good politician by definition is one who knows his opponent's worst statistical records. For example, at the Republican national convention of 1992 George Bush had less than an hour to address the nation. Within this time period he allotted to himself less than thirty seconds to attack the democratically controlled congress. Bush could have chosen five or ten figures to illustrate the poor performance of the Democrats. Instead he selected only one, but this one was a beauty. He fired a *bullet* with this figure. What did he say?

The loudest cry the Democrats were making in 1992 was that the Republicans caused the budget deficit. In similar words to these Bush stated, "these democrats in Congress gave themselves numerous pay raises during our recessionary times, so many in fact that it equals a 3,000% increase in pay for the house." This one statistic showed clearly that the democrats too were responsible for the budget deficit. How could they give themselves a 3,000% pay raise with taxpayer's hard earned money. Nobody gets a 3,000% pay hike! Bush used sound judgment in picking this figure. He could have chosen five or six statistics, but he wisely chose this one because it showed the Democrats in a <u>dim</u> <u>light</u>. Please be advised that I am not expressing my political views here. I am also not condoning Mr. Bush's method. I simply want you to see how important it is to choose a <u>significant</u> statistic. I don't know if 3,000% was an accurate statistic about Congress, but it was effective in supporting Mr. Bush's argument that evening.

Think hard about which statistics to highlight in your presentations? Find the one piece of data that *startles* people so they sit up and listen to you. Look for quality data, not quantity. Use your common sense in picking statistics and you will do fine.

Let's review the <u>second</u> step now: presenting data in *clear* language.

Once you have selected your numbers how do you present them effectively? The first point to remember is that not very many people understand statistics. Also remember that statistics is a boring subject to most folks. Your job as the speaker is to take this poorly understood and boring discipline and make it interesting. How do you achieve your objective? The answer is to present this strange information in clear language. Below are a few examples.

Foggy language

"This year market studies indicated that our Ford model escort did significantly better than the previous year in sales volume! In fact, we had a 7.5% increase in overall sales growth."

Clear language

"This year over 150,000 more American's chose to buy a Ford Escort than last year!"

Foggy language

"In this last business quarter the number of complaints dropped by 6% compared to the previous quarter."

SPEAKING YOUR BEST

Clear language

"Seven more happy customers left our store each day for the last three months, compared to the previous three month period."

Foggy language

"The statistics for our department reveal that our average expenditure per month is $67,456.00. This reflects a reduction of 5.6% over last year's average. We are cutting our costs!"

Clear language

"The bean counters tell me our department is saving over $3,000.00 a month compared to last year. We are cutting our costs folks!"

Can you see the difference between the foggy vs. clear examples? In the first example instead of using the percentage increase as a way of telling the audience that sales are up, the speaker used a better way. Saying "150,000.00" is more *concrete* than using the percentage 7.5%. We can almost visualize 150,000.00 cars, but how do you visualize 7.5%? Again in the second example the speaker chose to go with the whole number instead of the percentage. Computers understand percentages. People prefer concrete figures. Rather than saying that complaints dropped 6% the speaker elected to use the whole number seven. He also used the words, "more happy customers..." which is accentuating the positive instead of the negative. Another good idea was to say, "the last three months" in lieu of "this last business quarter." The last three months is a time period that sounds more *familiar* to people than the last business quarter.

In the third example the speaker refused to talk about percentages and averages which is language clear only to people comfortable with those terms. Why not get right to the point and say we are saving over $3,000.00 a month? The third example is shorter and more direct, both qualities <u>audiences</u> <u>appreciate</u>.

I want to make an important point here. If you know your audience is made up of people who understand percentages, means, and ratios then it's ok to use these statistical measures. Very often though, people will not know what you're talking about because they did poorly in math, or they forgot what they learned. Doesn't it make sense to express your statistics in <u>clear</u> <u>language</u> for these folks? I prefer using concrete illustrations even when my audience understands statistical measures because I think I'm more effective this way. Here is another example:

Foggy language

"You must consider that in the past five years our study has shown that over eight thousand people have died from aids. It's time we start doing something about it."

Clear language

"Let me show you how many people have died from aids in the last five years. If you laid out the dead bodies from head to toe, there would be a chain of corpses stretching three thousand miles from California to New York State. It's time we start doing something about it."

Which example makes a bigger impact? I feel the second one does because it uses *concrete* language to make a point. If you are more comfortable speaking in percentages, means, and ratios, by all means do so. The choice is a subjective one. Whichever method you choose though, make sure everyone in the audience gets your point. That is the objective of a *persuasive* presentation.

Summary

Do you understand how to present statistics now? The key is to present figures to your audience in clear and concrete language. If you are addressing accountants, then it's ok to speak about means, percentages and ratios. If you are talking to an audience that isn't familiar with these terms however, use *concrete* language they understand.

Using statistics wisely boils down to the two step formula. First, select which statistical data to highlight by carefully looking at who makes up your audience. Quality is more important than quantity. Choose a statistic that will make a dramatic impact. Second, talk about your numbers in language that people can easily grasp. Present your figures in *clear* language in lieu of foggy speech that obfuscates. Remember, your goal is not to sound like a statistician, but to deliver a clear and persuasive presentation. This two step formula requires some smart thinking on your part. Many speakers drown their audience with numbers and ruin their presentations. Choose significant figures for your audience and present them clearly. It's a simple two step formula that will help you be more *persuasive!* Good Luck!

Checklist

☑ Arithmetic mean (average)

☑ Percentages

☑ Ratios

☑ How to present your numbers.

☑ Foggy language vs. clear language

Chapter 9

Pathos, logos and ethos: secret elements for a stirring presentation

The degree to which you <u>connect</u> with people at the gut or emotional level marks the degree of your effectiveness. People are very sensitive creatures. They have feelings toward everything. If you deliver a presentation and don't target their feelings about the subject, you won't be *persuasive*. In addition to emotion (pathos), there are two other elements necessary for a successful presentation. You were probably taught these in high school but have forgotten them: logos and ethos. Sound familiar? Pathos means emotions. Logos means logic, and ethos means culture.

After reading this chapter you will understand how to apply these elements effectively. Whenever you hear a <u>stirring</u> presentation I guarantee these qualities are there. I advise you now to always look for them in your presentation.

Pathos

When you appeal to people's emotions you are applying the *pathos* element. Love, hate, pity, sympathy, respect, suspicion, fear, loyalty, jealously, affection, pride, hope and tenderness, to name a few. The list is endless because people are capable of feeling an incredibly wide range of emotions. That's the beauty of being human! In each delivery you make, no matter if it's two minutes or forty, you must reach people at this *emotional* or gut level to be persuasive. Here's an example:

Remember the presidential debates of 1992? In the final debate between Clinton, Perot and Bush one woman asked a question similar to this, "Have any of the candidates personally experienced hard times, and if not, how can you understand how to help us? Mr. Bush was the first to respond, and unfortunately for him, he did not respond to this woman's question at the gut level. He looked even worse on national T.V. because he didn't understand her question, and asked her to repeat it. To paraphrase this woman's question, she was asking, "Have you felt any *pain* from unemployment or financial loss to you or your loved ones in the last few years, and if not, how can you truly help us?" Bush missed the boat! He should have shown some sorrow or regret to make an emotional connection with this woman and the millions of Americans watching him. Instead he responded on an intellectual level only and loss votes. Clinton, on the other hand, moved from behind his lectern, walked right toward the woman and said "I know there are people out there hurting and I want to help them." Clinton displayed genuine emotion! He conveyed his sorrow, and, by doing so, acknowledged the *hard times* many Americans were going through. Clinton connected at the gut level with millions of Americans and won the debate. Bush confirmed what many Americans suspected: *he was out of touch!*

President Bush did not know how to be a persuasive speaker. He lost all the debates and the election because he could not connect with Americans emotionally. Clinton won the debates and the election because he applied all three elements.

Let's say you are a computer salesperson and you want to win a big account. You have the opportunity to sell 30 desktop computers to an important prospect. The only problem is that every other computer salesperson in town has the same opportunity. How are you going to beat the competition? One key is to target the emotions of your potential client. Let's say in your first meeting you discovered that *service* has been delivered poorly by the current vendor. You sensed the deep frustration felt by the management team because when their computers went down, it took one or two days before the vendor was out to fix them. In your presentation you should emphasize dramatically that service is the best quality about your company. I would say something like, "I'm not going to try and buffalo you, sometimes our computers will go down, everyone's does, but with our technical support team, you'll have two technicians at your office within two hours." I would stress this point again at the end of my presentation. I would say it with genuine emotion. I would win that account if the other salesperson failed to reach the prospect on an emotional level, all other criterion being equal.

Can you see the value of using pathos in your presentation? It's common sense to appeal to people's emotions. Be emotional in your talks. Target your audience where they live, in their hearts, and you'll be putting pathos into your presentation. Lets review the second element now.

Logos

Logos means logic. You'll have to appeal to people's minds to influence them too. Most speakers don't have much problem applying this element. High school and college train us to be logical. The only advice I'll give you about this element is organize your thoughts so that your audience can follow you easily. Don't give them too many facts and statistics. Your argument must be clear. Think hard about what it is you want to say and then find the simplest way to say it. Compare what you have to sell to your competitor and highlight his weaknesses. I personally like to solicit other people's opinions on the issues I'm facing, because often our discussions will help me gain valuable insight. You are never too smart not to benefit from the advice of others. Debate your point of view vigorously with a friend or your spouse. Let them play the devil's advocate. This type of competitive discussion will shore up any holes in your argument.

Another tip is to use unique analogies to get your point across. Analogies are effective because they can reach your audience concretely. With logos, you want to reach people's minds and the well thought out analogy will do that for you. For example, let's say you are delivering a presentation and trying to sell your company's software program. You might say something like this, "our software is completely menu driven. It's as easy to use as your T.V. sets at home." or how about this, "our customer service people are lonelier than the Maytag repair man." These type of analogies are extremely useful and help people understand complex subjects. Ross Perot was adept at using analogies. Remember this one, "if a business was run the way the federal government has been run, it would be in Chapter 11 today."

When you sit down to outline your presentation remember that good organization is critical. Let a bright friend play devil's advocate to test your reasoning. Use common sense and you'll do fine including *logos* in your presentation. Let's discuss the third and final element needed to deliver a stirring talk.

Ethos

Ethos is the least understood of the three elements to effective delivery. The American Heritage dictionary defines ethos as, "The disposition, character or attitude peculiar to a specific people, culture or group that distinguishes it from other peoples or groups; fundamental values or spirit; mores." I think this definition is a good one. When you are preparing to speak before a group you must understand their attitudes and dispositions. What education, habits or life experiences do they have in common? There are a lot of special interest groups out there. A computer programming department has an ethos all its own. The programmers usually have a free *spirited* culture, believing that as long as you work smart and write good software you can get away with idiosyncrasies. A lot of salespeople have flamboyant personalities, and they don't tolerate *shy* people because that attribute is a weakness in their profession. You have to appeal to your specific group's ethos to effectively influence them. Suppose you were talking to a group of ministers. Do you think a racial joke would get them to like you? Of course not! But I'll bet a racial joke would work with a group of bigots, unfortunately.

The trick to using *ethos* is understanding what the attitude and beliefs are of your audience, and then using this knowledge to bond with them. For example, people in California are generally more mellow than East Coasters. If you are from New York you might want to slow down the pace of your delivery to a California audience. If you will be addressing a religious congregation, you definitely don't want to use the Lord's name in vain. If you are speaking to a group of people who work in the same city, you can earn some popularity by complimenting the city in a positive way. How about if you were addressing a group of Republicans? I would dress conservatively and tell a joke showing I hate to pay taxes. *People like people who are like themselves.* That's why you have to understand your group's ethos, so you can <u>show</u> them you feel as they do.

I'll never forget the story my dad told me one time when I was preparing to interview for a job as a Claims Representative with the California State Automobile Association. He advised me to be careful not to say anything that goes against their beliefs. When I asked him what he meant he said that one time he was interviewing with the Philadelphia Gas and Electric company for an entry level job. He made it past the first interview. However, during the second and final interview the hiring manager asked him why he wanted to work for the gas company. My dad, being a recent immigrant from Ireland and not yet understanding the utility company's ethos replied, "What do you mean? I work for the money, don't you? He also responded alittle incredulously and this annoyed the interviewer. Later my dad found out from a friend that the Manager didn't hire him because he thought my dad wouldn't stay with the company very long, believing he was only looking to make some money and wasn't interested in a long future with Philadelphia Gas and Electric. Nothing could have been further from the truth! My dad had a wife and five kids at home. He wanted nothing more than the opportunity to work for a company with a future.

My dad didn't understand the *ethos* of a modern bureaucracy. He should have told the manager what he wanted to hear. He should have said what every mid-level manager in a large bureaucracy wants to hear, "I want to work for your company because I want to build a future for myself with a solid outfit. I have heard that your organization rewards people like me who work hard and are team players." Another good reply would have sounded like this, "I want to join a company with a future and my skills and experience could really help your department." Pop's ignorance cost him a good starting job with a stable utility company. (He did all right though, and eventually started his own company, but that's another story.) The point is you can't afford to make the same mistake. Think and understand what the *"disposition, character and attitude"* is of your listeners. You will deliver a more persuasive presentation this way.

An excellent example of how to apply *ethos* was given to us in the presidential race of 1992. Very few people knew who Ross Perot was before he ran, quit, and then reran for President of the United States. Yet, within a few months this man was the leading candidate for the job because he used pathos, logos, and ethos in all of his T.V. appearances. Perot used pathos with Americans by showing genuine disgust for federal waste. He was angry at the "career politicians" for causing the biggest budget deficit of the twentieth century. He talked of patriotism and made us feel *proud* to be Americans. This short man with his Texas accent c*onnected* with Americans at the gut level.

Mr. Perot applied logos with his infomercials. He presented to us graphs and pie charts supporting his arguments. He had a businessman's pragmatic answers to turning the economy around. He took the initiative by spending thirty minutes on national T.V. educating the public about sound financial principles.

Mr. Perot illustrated the ethos element better than any public official since Ronald Regan. Americans like people who give direct answers to direct questions. They like one-liners and epigrams. Perot was full of both. In contrast to Clinton and Bush who spoke like the kind of people they were, career politicians, the Texas billionaire spoke straight from the hip. Clinton and Bush would take three minutes to answer a yes or no question. Perot would answer the same question, in thirty seconds. He didn't dodge the question like a sophisticated politician. If a reporter asked him why his company lost money, Perot would answer, "because I made some mistakes." Americans loved Perot for his honest answers. He used ethos brilliantly because we felt Perot was just like us. He talked just like honest and hard working people do. In short, many Americans loved Perot because he was like them. If he hadn't quit the race and shown his indecisiveness, Perot might have been in the White House today. We might all be wearing boots, a ten gallon hat, and chewing tobacco.

How to use these elements

Now that you know the secret elements of a stirring presentation, how do you apply what you know? Good question! Let's take pathos first.

Pathos: There are two ways to use pathos. The <u>first</u> is to deliver your presentation with a lot of emotion. Be intense! People love people who are passionate about what they're doing. If your job is to sell fax machines, sell them like they were gold plated! Ask your listeners to buy your fax machines because they'll look back on their choice as the best decision they ever made. If you are a priest or a minister, get pumped up every Sunday and preach as if it will be your last day. If you are an executive or manager, inspire your employees to perform their best by being passionate when you speak to them. That's the first way to put some pathos into your presentation. The second way to use pathos was already mentioned in this chapter. Discover your audience's strongest emotions. Do they care more about saving money this year than getting quality? If so, then talk 75% about savings and 25% about quality. Are the decision makers you are selling to very cautious and conservative? If so, stress to them that you want them to take plenty of time before deciding. Give them names of conservative companies that currently use your product. Speak like a conservative 55 year old banker. Play detective and uncover what their strongest emotions are, and then target them in your presentation. These are the two ways to apply the *pathos* element effectively.

Logos: Think carefully about your argument or sales promotion. Why is your product better than the rest? Force yourself to think! Debate your argument with a bright friend and shore up any holes. Three of the best tips I will give you are the following: stay organized, stay organized, and stay very organized.

Ethos: Ask yourself a few questions. What type of people will be sitting and listening to you? How old are they? What part of the country are they from? How educated are they about your subject? Are they academics? Business people? Healthcare professionals? Politicians? High school parents? What are the attitudes these people have toward your subject?

These are the questions you must ask to adapt your talk to fit the needs of your audience. For example, if you're addressing academics you want to show respect for education and praise the virtues of study and higher level degrees. Talk about the brilliant engineering behind your product. If you are talking to business people, talk about bottom line and dependability. Speak about productivity, short term goals, and saving money since these are the age old criterion for business people. Learn what the favorite football team is of your decision makers and comment positively about them. Find out if your audience of three executives are *tennis* players or *softball* players. Learn how to show your listeners that you share similar interests. *They will like you more if you are more like them*. Define your audience, analyze them, and then use this information to bond with them.

Summary

Look for the *pathos, logos* and *ethos* elements in your presentations. Target your audience's emotions, be emotional in your delivery, and present your argument in an organized manner. Show people that you share common values so you can bond with them. These three ingredients are the recipe for a stirring presentation. *Good luck!*

Checklist

☑ Pathos

☑ Logos

☑ Ethos

Chapter 10

Vocabulary: building your word power

Why is it necessary to think about words? Because you are what you speak! People base their perception of you on many things. Body language, voice quality, eye contact, enthusiasm and facial expression are very important. But word choice and the context in which you apply them show people how *intelligent* you are. How often have you watched a popular actor sitting on a TV talk show look incredibly sharp until they began speaking, then they sounded like a high school drop out? The reason they don't impress you is that their ability to express themselves is not as powerful when they lack a good script. They fumble their words and sentences because they have a limited vocabulary.

I don't mean to pick on Actors. Some of them are very smart people. My perception of Arnold Schwarzenegger was that he was a big dumb weightlifter until I heard him speak on a TV talk show. After listening to him it became clear that he is a bright guy.

We are all guilty of weak vocabularies now and then because applying good word skills, like applying any skill, requires regular study and practice to be effective at it. Can you imagine super Tennis Pro Pete Sampras being effective if he didn't study and practice his craft each day? Of course not! We have to study and practice to be good at it. Most of us have to work for a living forty or fifty hours a week. This work is very often repetitive, non creative, and it doesn't require us to think and build our word power. Hence our vocabularies, and our ability to express ourselves intelligently is poor because we are rusty. Let's discuss now how you can build and maintain a *marvelous* vocabulary.

Phase one: read challenging books and articles

What's your primary source of new information? Sadly, for most Americans it's TV. Too many people who were good achievers in high school and college have lost their academic prowess because now they watch only TV movies and news shows. If you add up all the hours of TV the average person has watched in their lifetime, the figure would be frightening. My guess is that it would be two or three years of TV watching! *Two or three years*! Does this scare you? It frightens me! Watching TV is a passive activity and the quality of 95% of television isn't even challenging to the intellect of high school dropouts.

The first phase to improving your vocabulary then is to STOP watching so much TV. It is literally killing your brain. You must also start reading challenging books and articles. It doesn't matter what subjects you read as long as they are intellectually challenging for you. You can read mystery novels, romance, horror, sci-fi, biographies, how-to books. Any fiction or nonfiction book is worth reading if it is written well and forces you to think. Read books that pertain to your profession. Take night courses in your line of work. Most companies in America will reimburse your tuition for night school, if it is related to your profession. It doesn't matter, though, if you want to read something totally unrelated to your profession. Hobbies benefit us because they offer a completely different type of stimulation than our jobs. The important point is that you *read* books that are challenging for your mind and bring joy to your spirit.

Get into the habit of reading stimulating magazine articles too. If you don't already, subscribe now to a good magazine. Reader's Digest is an excellent choice because it contains articles full of wisdom and common sense. It even has a section on building your vocabulary. You must also choose which newspaper you will read on a regular basis. Look for a newspaper with a reputation for quality reporting and indepth articles. This paper may not be a big city publication. A lot of our major metropolitan dailies are surprisingly dull and written to appeal to people's base interests. Search for any regional, prestigious publication. Whatever type of reading you do make sure it is challenging, and make sure you read at least a half hour each night. You must read more on the weekends - at least a couple of hours. The next paragraph will give you tips on <u>remembering</u> the words that you read.

Whenever you discover a new word in your reading, examine it closely. Understand the context in which it is being used and look it up in the dictionary. Now try using the word in a sentence to confirm that you truly understand it. By taking these steps you won't forget the word and will probably begin using it in your everyday parlance.

The first step to building your vocabulary and educating yourself is to STOP watching TV and start reading challenging books and articles. Take the first step now!

Phase two: start writing regularly

Remember writing your papers in high school and college? They were challenging to complete on time and get that cherished A+. One way you can increase your vocabulary and sharpen your mind is by writing a couple of hours each weekend. Writing is a natural partner to reading when it comes to strengthening your mind. Writing forces your brain to think! Quality reading is also a friend of writing because your writing reflects how bright you are. The more you read good literature the brighter you'll be than those *boob tube* watchers.

What can you write? If you're not a syndicated columnist or a correspondent for a major magazine you can still keep a diary. Many intelligent people keep diaries. A diary helps you *examine* your life. The decisions that you make, the behaviors you exhibit, and the direction your life is taking can be improved upon by writing a diary. Why? Because writing forces you to *think* through the issues! It's one thing to sit on the couch and think about your daily experiences, but if you sit down at a desk and write about it, you will be surprised at how *clearly* you see things. Try keeping a diary for a month as an experiment! You will be surprised at the results it will have for your own *understanding.*

What else can you write? If you like to show initiative at work, it would behoove you to write out your ideas before presenting them to your superiors. You can also write short articles, glossaries or checklists for your staff or fellow employees. For example, I work full time as an insurance Adjuster. In my third year I became an expert in many aspects of my job. I decided to show some initiative by helping the younger adjusters, so I wrote a checklist of forms that we use daily. My checklist saved each adjuster valuable time because they could simply refer to my checklist, in lieu of dragging out a *big manual* each time they needed a form. Another way I showed initiative was by writing a glossary of medical terms used by physical therapists. A lot of these terms were alien to us until I researched them and created my easy-to-read glossary. I created these opportunities to practice my writing skills and they benefited both my career and my co-workers.

What else can you write? You can do what I've done! You could write a book on a subject you know a lot about and in which you have a keen interest. Writing a book is a terrific way to enhance your writing skills because you get better with every new page you write. It also improves your vocabulary because, to make your book entertaining to read, you need to use lively words with emotional impact. You don't have to write an entire book either; a brief booklet on your area of expertise could be valuable to novices.

There are many reasons to write and you can create an opportunity by thinking about what needs are currently not met in your field. Writing is another smart way to build your vocabulary and give your mind the regular *work out* it needs to stay in shape. The choice is yours, my friend. Writing could be your ticket to self improvement and career advancement.

Phase three: join social clubs

Why? There are plenty of good reasons. You will learn new words from other people you meet in the club. You will also be forced to speak and defend your opinions in front of others. In clubs you also get to meet new people which is a very stimulating experience. You can get your spiritual needs met too if it's a *supportive* club.

Clubs are good for your self esteem because they give you a sense of identity. The more active you become in your club, the more self confidence you build. Clubs are also great for sharpening your elocutionary skills when you hold a leadership position in them.

There are a lot of clubs out there to join. Here is a partial list of some to assist you finding one in your town: hiking clubs, book review clubs, dance studios, lecture meetings, bird watching, whale watching, nature walks, poetry clubs, tennis and racquet ball clubs, volley ball and softball leagues, golf clubs, religious groups, civic organizations, etc, etc. As you can see, there are thousands of special interests groups out there. What are your interests? *Go* join a club that shares them.

I belong to a public speaking club called **Toastmasters International**. This organization has clubs in almost every city in America. We meet every Tuesday night at a local church-owned building. I have learned an unbelievable number of new words at my club. I highly recommend this organization for you to develop your presentation skills too. The club dues are inexpensive and you learn here what some companies pay thousands of dollars to teach their executives.

Phase four: play words games for fun

The fourth exercise you can do to increase your vocabulary is play word games like Scrabble or the crossword puzzles in your local newspaper. These games are fun and they are a *veritable* gold mine of English words. You can play these games as a substitute for watching TV. I guarantee you will see a marked improvement in your vocabulary and intellect when you switch off the tube and turn your mind toward playing these games.

Summary

"Garbage in, garbage out" is what my dad always told me. He would say this anytime he saw me staring at the boob tube. When your primary source of new information is the boob tube, how bright can you be?

If you don't feed your mind by studying, reading, and experiencing life, it will be as stale as the television box. When you speak before others the bigger your vocabulary the better you can choose the right word to get your meaning across. People like listening to an educated person speak who can apply unique words they don't hear very often. You can be that educated person but you have to work at it.

Some of you are out of school, and are working, so there are no more classes or teachers to help you learn new words, or to force you to read challenging books and articles. You must do it yourself. It is easy to do once you get into the habit of doing it. Well, what are you doing tonight? Watching TV or *learning*?

Checklist

☑ Phase one: read challenging books and articles

☑ Phase two: start writing regularly

☑ Phase three: join social clubs

☑ Phase four: play word games for fun

Chapter 11

Tips for special occasions

This final chapter will spark your imagination about what to say on those special occasions like presenting awards to employees, accepting awards, toasting friends at wedding anniversaries, birthdays, graduations, and other milestone events. Always speak from the heart at these affairs. Always keep your speech short, especially if it's before a meal. If you are bestowing an honor on someone else, don't steal the spotlight too much! On the other hand, you don't want to look like a witless friend, and that's why reading this chapter will benefit you. You will sound a lot more intelligent when you say the right words with style. Apply the fundamentals of good presenting that you have learned in this book: good body posture, strong eye contact, speaking slowly, and closing with a clear message. Remember people are watching you too! Read this chapter and discover the secrets to toasting others.

Presenting an award

The most important thing to say when presenting an award is describing to your listeners the reason this person is being singled out as an achiever. Tell your audience how successful this person was at doing at their job. Point out how few people reach their level. Highlight their significant accomplishments. You have to keep it short but *meaningful*. If this person faced any unusual obstacles such as a poor sales territory, or a huge workload, tell this to your listeners. You don't have to be a windbag or a hero worshipper, but give this person the credit he or she has earned. Here are a few examples to show you how it's done:

"Bob is sitting at the head of the table here today because he sold more software programs than anyone else this year. I know he faced stiff competition too, because many of you salespeople had great years, and we deeply appreciate it! Bob, I know you're going to like your prize because you love playing golf. I have in my hand a gift certificate to RJ's sporting goods store in the amount of $1,000.00. Bob, from all of us, thanks for your outstanding performance in 1993."

The above award speech is brief but meaningful. It delivers a clear message that management really rewards top performers. The speaker also complimented the other salespeople to avoid any acrimony in the group. Here's another example:

"Staci Schwartz has been the driving force behind our company's marketing success. Her ideas, personality and management experience are the reason we captured 11% of the frozen yogurt market in California this year. One of the best talents this women has is her ability to inspire others around her to perform their best. Two of her staff earned promotions this year, thanks in part to her support. That's why it gives me great pleasure, Staci, to present to you the employee of the year award. Congratulations and thanks from all of us!"

This speech illustrates a nice technique to use when presenting an award. The presenter pointed out that even though Staci Schwartz has the marketing smarts to excel in her job, she is also a supportive team player and cares about her people. Whenever you are giving out an award it shows class to comment on the winner's human side too. You will be respected tremendously for making this moment uplifting and unforgettable.

What is the secret to presenting awards with style? Keep it brief but very meaningful, highlight any unusual obstacles the award recipient overcame, and to make it truly memorable, show the winner's human side to warm up the audience.

Accepting an award

What do you say when you're the one accepting the award? One approach that is universally popular, and the one I recommend is best summarized in this word: humility! Audiences respect people who have earned a promotion or an award and then are humble about their accomplishments. Here's an example:

"Salespeople can not be successful if the company they are working for doesn't support them, and I wouldn't have accomplished what I did this year if I didn't receive the support from my sales manager, Mike Hartzel. Mike is the ideal sales manager because he always listens to me when I need support. His ideas and feedback, as well as his willingness to join me in the field, made my job that much easier. I also want to thank our customer service staff who field the problem calls. I have a lot of accounts that keep buying because of you guys and gals. Thanks also to our marketing staff whose advertising efforts brought in a ton of good leads this year. I accept this award on everyone's behalf and look forward to another big year!"

The speaker did the one thing every award winner must do to be effective with the audience. He thanked everyone who played a role in his success. You should do the same. Remember to thank others and show a little humility when you receive an award. You'll earn respect for your wisdom this way.

What's the secret to accepting an award effectively? *Show humility!* By letting the audience see that your head hasn't expanded to blimpish proportions, you are presenting yourself as a poised and well adjusted human being.

Introducing other Speakers

You will at some time be called upon to introduce other speakers, friends, and work associates to an audience. Here are a few tips to help you introduce someone with style and effectiveness.

When you introduce another speaker you have three goals: your *first* is telling your listeners what this person is going to be talking about. *Second,* tell them why this person is qualified to speak on the subject. And *third,* tell a witty anecdote about the speaker to warm up the audience. This third goal is your most important one. You set the required mood for your speaker so they can meet a receptive audience. The mood you set is dependent upon your speaker's subject. If it will be a lighthearted talk, then you might want to say something funny to loosen up the crowd. If the subject is serious, set the right tone by displaying gravity. Let's say your speaker is going to give a talk about sales performance standards and single out individual achievers. Your best technique is to remind everyone how vitally important it is that someone sells your products. You might say something like this:

"All the great effort we spend to build the best computers in the business would be in vain if we couldn't sell them. Pat McLaughlin manages our sales force in California. Pat has been instrumental in getting us into the insurance market. His sales team has outsold every other division in the company for the past two years. Pat, why don't you come up here and tell us which salespeople kicked butt for you this year!"

The tone of this introduction is sober respect and admiration. Now the audience is prepared to hear more success stories about these dynamic salespeople. You can also see the other two key goals that were accomplished in this introduction: the audience is told what this speaker is going to talk about and why he is qualified to speak on the subject. The individual who gave this introduction did an excellent job.

Here's another example. Let's say you are called upon to introduce a new hire. You might say something like this:

"Before I introduce Tom Little, our new Operations Manager, I want to tell you that I grabbed him from our biggest competitor because he won a promotion for doing what I hired him to do for our company: save money. Tom is going to tell us a little bit about his background and experience in Operations."

Again in this example, the tone set is one of respect. This tone is the one you most often hear in the corporate workplace. Do you see the other two key goals accomplished in this introduction too? The first sentence tells them why he is qualified to speak on the subject, namely, he earned a promotion for saving money at another company. The last sentence informs the audience what this speaker will say.

Remember, even though you are not the main speaker, you want to look smart too. Let you personality shine through as you talk. Keep your body posture tall and articulate your words clearly. Be enthusiastic. The best introductions are always the most animated.

In summary, you must achieve *three* key goals in your introduction: *one*, tell them what the speaker will say. *Two,* tell them why this person is qualified to speak on the subject, and *three,* set the appropriate tone to prepare the audience. Organize your introduction with these three goals in mind and you will be successful.

Birthdays

The real message behind your toast to a friend or relative on their birthday is that they are loved very much. You can talk about your relationship over the years, emphasizing how your friend was always there when you needed him or her. You can tell a story from the past about some rough times you went through, and your family member's or your friend's instrumental efforts to help out. The best piece of advice I can share with you about speaking at these occasions is to let your heart be your guide. It is sometimes difficult in our American culture for us to express our love and respect for each other, but a birthday is the perfect opportunity to do so. You can use this formal occasion as an excuse to tell someone how much you care for them. Here's an example:

"I know that we haven't been able to spend a lot of time together in recent years because you're in New York and my wife and I are living in California, but I want you to know that having a big sister like you to look after me when I was young really meant a lot to me. Here's thinking of you sis."

Here's another example:

"I met this guy about two years ago because we are both addicted tennis players and we have probably played over one hundred matches together. Brian, you've been a good loser and a sore loser over the years. When are you going to learn how to play the game? Just kidding. What I really want to say is that our friendship is more important to me than who wins or loses on the court. Here's a drink to you buddy! Lets stay friends in the 90's."

What is the secret to toasting someone on their birthday? Speak from your heart! Don't be afraid to show some feeling! We don't get too many opportunities in our culture to show people how much they mean to us, so use their birthdays as an excuse to let them know how much you care.

Anniversaries

There are two common types of anniversaries: employee anniversaries and your parent's or friend's wedding anniversaries. Let me give you some tips about what to say on these memorable occasions.

Employee anniversaries

Employees who are celebrating their fifth, tenth, fifteenth or more years of employment with a company want to hear a big thank you for staying with the organization. As their manager, you must say a few words that shows how much you appreciate his or her dedicated years of service. If the employee is an outstanding achiever, then highlight his or her career accomplishments. If he or she has been an average or below average player, try and find some unique contribution they make to your department. The contribution may simply be their friendly personality. Here's an example:

"Our department has always felt like a second home for many of us, thanks to Janet McBride's willingness to listen and care. You have made our department a happy place for us to come to each day. Thanks for all your dedicated years of service. Janet, we look forward to another twenty!"

Keep your tone of voice upbeat and sincere. Express your sentiments with a smile and you will make the employees and everyone's day meaningful.

Wedding anniversaries

Wedding anniversaries can be very important events for the two spouses. Usually the fifth, tenth, fifteenth and twentieth year are celebrated with the most notoriety (the same as our employment years; now that's a scary analogy). If you are given the honor of toasting your two parents or your best friend, you should keep the following thoughts in mind.

When two people are happy together it is definitely an event worth celebrating. Any couple that stays together in a happy marriage for many years must love each other very much. You can capture this fact by saying something like this:

"I would like to offer a toast to Mary and Jamie. They have built a family of four over the past fifteen years and by all accounts they are still going strong. They are a shinning example to us that when two people love each other and are willing to work at their relationship, harmony results. Best of luck to you two. Let's lift up our glasses to these happily married folks!"

The above toast has two qualities all great toasts have: it is short and meaningful. You might want to celebrate, not only the couple's love for each other, but the institution of marriage as well. Here's another example:

"When Joe and Dorothy met, Eisenhower was President. These two lovebirds have been married for thirty-five years. Congratulations from all of us to you two tonight! I am glad I have known both of you as friends and neighbors. You have brought a lot of happiness into my life. Turn on the TV and you see programs showing people getting divorced all the time. Your love and respect for each other over the last thirty-five years proves that marriage is a good institution when two adults enter it with both feet on the ground. Everyone please join me in raising your glasses to Joe and Dorothy and saluting their love and commitment to each other. Here's to you two kids."

My advice for you about organizing your thoughts to offer a wedding anniversary toast is think about one clear point you want to make, and then focus your words to express this point. I used this method in the above two examples. In the first toast my key point was that Mary and Jamie love each other very much. What is my key point in the second example? Simply, that marriage is a good institution. I have been at too many anniversaries where the person giving the toast fumbled for the right words. Take a few moments to organize your thoughts to express one key point. Apply this technique and you will deliver a meaningful message to your parents or close friends.

Graduations

What should you say to someone graduating from college, law, medical school or who just earned their MBA? My feeling is that there are two parts to an effective graduation toast. The first part congratulates the graduate on a job well done. The second part wishes this person a bright future. Here's an example:

"Brian, you have been sacrificing your weekends for the past three years to earn your MBA. Congratulations buddy. You did it! I know that with your ambition and now with this degree under your belt your future will be full of success. Everyone, please join me in drinking a toast to Brian."

Use your imagination to come up with complimentary words on this occasion to deliver a custom toast to your friend or family member. Congratulate them for a job well done and wish them future success.

Funerals

The most important advice about giving a eulogy is one we all instinctively know: speak from your heart. What you say on these occasions is entirely your decision, but I can give you some tips on organizing your sentiments. The average time people expect you to speak is about fifteen minutes. This gives you time to say many things about the deceased person. The traditional approach and the one I recommend is to organize your talk chronologically. Start at your relative's youth if you're old enough to know it. If it's your parent, you can begin in your childhood. Say a few words about what your relative accomplished. Tell a meaningful story that shows how much this person was admired or loved. Here's one example to open a eulogy.

"My Dad came to America as an immigrant in 1956, when he was thirty-six years old. That's an age when most men are settling down for good. He came with little money, only a high school education, and few friends. He started his own home improvement business and by the end of his second year in America, he was making enough money to purchase a house, and send for his wife and four kids. I guess you could say my dad was a pioneer. He and Mom raised five kids in a foreign land at a time when the Irish were a minority. When I was a kid growing up in Philadelphia my dad was always there for me. I remember an incident when I was thirteen. A man smacked me *hard* in the face because I was riding my motor bike in the neighborhood. I guess the motor noise stressed him out. I came home crying. Dad went into a rage when he found out what happened. He raced two blocks and found this guy. My two brothers and half a dozen neighbors were close behind. My Dad got in this guy's face and asked him, *"Is it true that you laid a hand on my son?"* This guy was about thirty two. My Dad was over fifty, but I could tell Dad wasn't thinking about his age. He was only mad as hell that a stranger had struck his son. Fortunately, this guy apologized and no blows were exchanged. I never forgot that event, even though it happened over twenty years ago and was over in less than two minutes. You see, from that day forward I always knew that my Dad loved me, and would defend me, no matter what the risk was to his personal safety." *(True story)*

The above opening is a good example of organizing your talk chronologically and sharing a powerful story about your loved one. From this point you can describe the many things your parent or relative did for you over the years. I would discuss how they influenced you in positive ways. You can now move on to more recent years and share with everyone your special feelings for the deceased. A good way to close out your eulogy using the chronological method would be to tell everyone what the last wishes were of your relative. You could simply say that your relative wants everyone to continue to be a close knit family. You could also issue a request to siblings to lead productive, healthy, and happy lives. Whatever sentiments you feel are appropriate, to keep it organized chronologically, I recommend closing out your speech with some comments about the present and future. Here's an example:

In closing, I know that my dad wanted his sons, daughters and his close friends to continue living their lives to the fullest. Be hard working and hard playing! Have fun and laugh a lot! Always expect to give more than you expect to get! Plan for the future but smell the roses today! Continue to educate yourselves about our changing world. Be there for your relatives and friends when they need you. Watch over them and keep evil out of their lives. Demand a lot from yourself and this world because you only have one life to live. And finally, be a *tenacious* fighter until your last breath is gone! God bless you all!

You will know what to say at these sad and yet joyful occasions. Organize a eulogy talk chronologically, and you will express yourself clearly.

Checklist

☑ Presenting an award

☑ Accepting an award

☑ Introducing other speakers

☑ Birthdays

☑ Anniversaries

☑ Employee anniversaries

☑ Wedding anniversaries

☑ Graduations

☑ Funerals

Bibliography

1. Cook, Jeff Scott: *The Elements of Speechwriting and Public Speaking.* Macmillion Publishing, 1991.

2. Hamlin, Sonya: *How To Talk So People Listen.* Harper & Row, 1990.

3. Fletcher, Leon: *How To Speak Like A Pro.* Ballantine Books, 1983.

4. Wohlmuth, Ed: *The Overnight Guide To Public Speaking.* Penquin Books, 1993.

5. Parkhurst, William: *The Eloquent Executive.* Avon Books, 1990.

6. Robinson, James: *Better Speeches In Ten Simple Steps.* Prima Publishing and Communications, 1989.

7. Carnegie, Dale: *How To Develop Self-Confidence And Influence People By Public Speaking.* Pocket Books, 1956.

8. Drummond, Mary-Ellen: *Fearless And Flawless Public Speaking With Power, Polish, And Pizazz.* Pfeiffer & Company, 1993.

9. Wilder, Claudyne: *The Presentations Kit.* John Wiley & Sons, 1991.

10. Mandel, Steve: *Effective Presentation Skills.* Crisp Publications, 1993.

11. Frank, Milo: *How To Get Your Point Across In 30 Seconds Or Less.* Pocket Books, 1987.

speed	*34*
statistics	*1, 8, 10 - 12, 15, 17, 19, 41, 43, 66, 71, 75 - 80, 86*
story	*4 - 7, 17 - 18, 44, 88 - 89, 108, 113 - 114*

T

transitions	*3, 9*

V

visual aids	*57 - 58, 61 - 62*
vocabulary	*43, 95 - 99, 101*
vocal variety	*34 - 36*
voice	*32 - 36, 49, 51, 53 - 54, 95, 110*
	speed *34*
	voice tone *27*
	volume *33 - 34, 53*

W

wakes people up	*4*
wisdom	*12, 43, 97, 106*
witty	*6 - 7, 18, 39, 46, 52, 106*
words	*3 - 4, 11, 23, 27, 30, 43, 49, 52 - 54, 58 - 60, 62, 76, 78, 95, 97, 99 - 101, 103, 108, 110, 112 - 113*

Incredible side effects and Toastmasters International

In my opinion, the best benefit from giving presentations are the *incredible side effects* you will feel. What am I talking about? Speaking before a group is a very *stimulating* experience. It forces you to think clearly and builds your self confidence. Expressing yourself before a group is also good for your heart. It's a *catharsis!* When you tell people what is on your mind it feels pretty darn good. If you have the opportunity to speak before groups on a regular basis you're lucky! If you don't have this opportunity, there is another way to get these incredible side effects that will energize you.

Join any local Toastmaster's club in your town. Toastmasters is an international speaking organization that has been around since the 1920's. Joining a local speaking club will give you the chance to deliver presentations in front of a supportive and captive audience. You can practice one night a week and get immediate feedback. I guarantee your presentation skills will improve quickly. You will also feel your self confidence grow by *leaps* and *bounds*. Club dues are inexpensive compared to the thousands of dollars some companies pay for the same training. These clubs are a terrific place to meet new people and build friendships too! Join a club and watch how the *incredible side effects* boost your self confidence, and renew your spirit.

ABOUT THE AUTHOR

Kevin Boland has been speaking before live audiences for over ten years. He holds a B. A. degree from U. C. Berkeley, in political studies. He began his business career in 1985 as a sales representative for MCI Tele-communications. In only two years, he was promoted to Senior Account Executive and earned top honors in MCI's west coast sales division. In 1987 he joined the marketing group of a start-up software developer called Berkeley Softworks. At this company, he polished his presentation skills further by giving talks to computer-user groups. His popularity as a speaker was so great, that one trade show promoter paid him $500.00 to deliver a one hour presentation. Mr. Boland is also a member in good standing at Toastmaster's International, the world's largest group of public speakers. He speaks competitively and in 1995 won Toastmaster's International Area Speech contest in Marin County, California. Kevin believes strongly that public speaking builds self-confidence and sharpens your mental faculties. His advice for speakers is simple, "learn the basics first - vocal variety, organization, eye contact, posture, and gestures - master these and you will quickly be an effective speaker."